D0190661

Campsite Memories
True Tales from Wild Places

by Cliff Jacobson
Illustrations by Cliff Moen

ICS BOOKS, Inc.
Merrillville, Indiana

Dedication

To Leonard "Lenny" Schwartz—
friend, colleague, humanitarian, and the best school principal
I have ever known. Thank you, Lenny,
for giving so much of yourself to all of us.

recycled paper

All ICS titles are printed on 50% recycled paper from
pre-consumer waste. All sheets are processed without
using acid.

PUBLISHED BY:
ICS Books, Inc.
1370 E. 86th Place
Merrillville, IN 46410
800-541-7323

Library of Congress Cataloging-in-Publication Data
Jacobson, Cliff.
    Campsite memories: true tales from wild places /
Cliff Jacobson; illustrations by Cliff Moen.
        p. cm.
    Includes index.
    ISBN: 0-934802-88-2: $9.99
        1. Canoes and canoeing—Minnesota. 2. Canoes and canoeing—
Canada. 3. Adventure and adventurers—Minnesota. 4. Adventure and
adventurers—Canada. I. Title.
GV776.M6J33 1994   93-48780
797.1'22'09776—dc20   CIP

Introduction

THE GREAT ARCTIC EXPLORER, Vilhjalmur Steffanson, on return from one of his many expeditions, once was asked if he'd had any adventures.

"No—no adventures, just experiences!" Steffanson replied, politely adding, "Adventures are the result of incompetence."

Maybe so. But nature rears its unpredictable head so frequently, and with such diversity, that even those who are highly skilled and well prepared occasionally suffer the trauma of "adventure." In fact, it is the uncertainty of the wilderness experience that encourages us to explore new horizons. Challenged by our own curiosity, we ponder the dotted lines on maps and fantasize about what lies over the mountain and around the bend. Perhaps, as Steffanson suggests, adventures and fools do go hand in hand. But dreams are the real stuff of adventuring, the impetus that drives us beyond the beaten path.

The stories in this book are all true. Most began with a dream and a conscientious study of maps and logistics. Others, as Steffanson would suggest, are true "adventures." The majority of accounts are from my own experiences as a professional canoe guide in Minnesota and Canada. A few stories are based on accounts from close friends whose testimony I trust. There's a mixture of humor, joy, sadness, tragedy and testable morality—plus the essence of "wildness" and the fulfillment of dreams. I hope you enjoy reading *Campsite Memories* as much as I loved writing it.

Try These Other Books By
Cliff Jacobson

- The Basic Essentials of Camping
- The Basic Essentials of Canoeing
- The Basic Essentials of Solo Canoeing
- The Basic Essentials of Map & Compass
- The Basic Essentials of Knots for the Outdoors
- The Basic Essentials of Trailside Shelter
- The Basic Essentials of Cooking in the Outdoors
- Camping Secrets
- Camping's Forgotten Skills
- Canoeing and Camping Beyond the Basics
- Canoeing Wild Rivers 2nd Edition

Available from your favorite bookstore or outdoor retailer. For a complete list of ICS BOOKS titles

Call Toll Free 1-800-541-7323

Table of Contents

The Wilberforce Falls Affair
Tripping Into Marriage on the Hood River

W HEN ADVENTURER SUE HARINGS graduated from college in
1971, she set out to explore the world alone. A middle-
school teacher from River Falls, Wisconsin, Susie has scuba-dived
off the Great Barrier Reef, hiked in Australia, New Zealand, Grand
Cayman Island and the Orient, as well as Alaska and Montana's
Glacier National Park, and has paddled scores of wild rivers in
Minnesota and Canada. Competent, friendly and charming, 46-
year-old Susie is at home wearing pile and Green Wellie boots, or
all dolled up in "girl clothes." Dubbed "FRU" (Frivolous,
Ridiculous, Unnecessary) queen of the Minnesota Canoe
Association because she brings too much gear on all her trips (but
to her credit carries it all), Susie ties passion-pink surveying ribbon to everything she owns. That, and her infectious smile, are her
trademarks.

"I like to be feminine and have pretty things around me," says
Susie. "I won't go anywhere without my earrings and makeup!"

I met Susie in 1986, when she joined a canoe trip I was leading
for the Science Museum of Minnesota. She proved to be a capable
paddler and amiable partner. Her smiling, upbeat nature earned her
the respect of the crew and the title of "trip clown." When I would
call her a "forty-year-old teen-ager" or a "walking garage sale,"
she would simply smile coyly and say something clever, which
would bring tears of laughter to everyone. Susie refused to grow
up: She screamed in the rapids, laughed during thunderstorms,
and, like a little kid, did everything possible to get out of camp
chores. She was the hit of the party and everyone loved her.

Years passed, and our friendship and respect for one another
grew. Our relationship centered around canoeing and camping and

was purely platonic. I was happily married to Sharon and Susie liked—no loved—her single, flirtatious lifestyle. Susie knew I loved my wife and did not fool around. I knew that married men did not exist in her life. We were just good friends, pure and simple.

Then, on December 11, 1990, tragedy struck. Sharon suffered a massive asthma attack and died on our living room floor. She was barely fifty years old. For the next two months, I wallowed in self-pity. Both kids were away at college, my ten-year-old Shelty dog had died a month earlier, and for the first time in twenty-four years I was completely alone. I missed Sharon so much. I needed to love again, to smile again. I needed the touch and warmth of a woman. Admittedly, Susie was not my first choice to date: she was too much a friend—one I didn't think I could get serious about. But I desperately needed her happy smile, so I asked her to dinner at a fine Italian restaurant.

From then on, we became constant companions, sharing one adventure after another. Together, we walked the snow-draped trail to Devils Den on the Kinnikinic River, broke March ice in our solo canoes, snowshoed the outback during a blizzard, winter-camped along Lake Superior, and hiked a mile into the woods at midnight to sleep near a wolf den.

Ten months after our first date, Susie agreed to marry me . . . that is, on condition that the wedding take place on another great adventure.

Susie knew I would be leading a canoe trip down the Hood River in the Northwest Territories of Canada during the summer of 1992, so she begged to go along. The highlight of the trip was Wilberforce Falls—an awesome cataract that drops 160 feet through a three mile canyon. The highest waterfall north of the Arctic Circle, Wilberforce would be a perfect wedding site. "I'll wear a fur-trimmed wedding dress and my Green Wellies," giggled Susie.

I liked the idea, but unfortunately, the trip was filled and there was no space for a bride. We considered chartering a float plane to carry her from Yellowknife (capitol of the Northwest Territories) to Wilberforce Falls, 350 air miles away, but when costs were computed, it was out of the question. The one feasible option was to put her aboard the weekly commuter flight from Yellowknife to Bathurst Inlet Lodge on the Arctic Ocean. From there, lodge owner Glen Warner could fly her about 40 air miles to a tundra lake three miles from the falls. Susie would pack her wedding dress, accouterments and nonessential "FRU" across the tundra to the marriage site, where she would wait alone for two days until we arrived by canoe. "It'll be my most remote solo trip!" grinned Susie.

Fortunately, just weeks before the great adventure, a man dropped out of the expedition and Susie was able to join the crew. She was the only woman among nine men, but it didn't bother her at all, even when she discovered that her bridesmaid would have to be male.

Destination: Yellowknife, Northwest Territories, 2,311 miles from River Falls, Wisconsin. Five people in a van and forty-six hours of non-stop driving. The pavement stops at the MacKenzie River. From here to the territorial capitol, you eat dust, road oil and fist-sized gravel. Graders are an endangered species: flat tires, flying stones and oil-caked mud are not. The sign, "Welcome to Yellowknife," is welcomed!

First stop, the only car wash in town. Thirty Canadian dollars buys enough bug- and tar-remover, scrub brushes and time to make the rig touchable. With eight pairs of hands working, the wash job takes just thirty minutes. Then, it's off to Air Tindi, where float plane service into the Hood River system has been arranged for more than a year. Over the growl of a landing Twin Otter, dispatcher Bill Gawletz, who has a genuine liking for canoeists, hails a hearty welcome to our crew. Plans are finalized; Sixteen-thousand Canadian dollars change hands, and takeoff is scheduled for 7 A.M. tomorrow.

A shower and nap at the Discovery Inn and it's off to experience the wonders of Yellowknife. There's Eskimo and Indian art to buy, a wondrous museum to see and, for Susie and I and marriage commissioner Charles LeFevere, a date with the marriage division of "Vital Statistics."

A pretty young lady named Vickie Joan Hickey enthusiastically ushers us into her office. There are forms to sign and fees to pay, and in the end, it's legal. Charlie is certified to perform the wedding on August 12, 1992. The signings and instructions take about an hour. Though the Northwest Territories is about one-fifth the size of the United States, there are only 55,000 inhabitants, most of which live in Yellowknife and surrounding "southern" communities. People—especially priests and ministers—are rare above the tree line. That's why there are marriage commissioners—the priests aren't always where you need them.

At 10 A.M. on August 1, two Twin Otter float planes settle into a quiet bay above the first rapid on the Hood River. It's raining and confusion abounds. Thank God there are no bugs! Minutes later, having disgorged its cargo, the plane revs for takeoff. There are waves and long solemn looks and the customary last fly-over. Packs are muscled into canoes and brightly colored nylon splash covers are attached. "Where's the wedding pack?" I call. Dead silence. Again, "Where's the wedding pack?"

"Okay, you guys, who hid it? Who's the clown . . . It's not funny!" yells Susie, hysterically. Again, no answer. Susie and I exchange doleful looks: the white canvas pack that contains her ermine-trimmed wedding dress, a guaranteed-to-stay-fresh-for-a-month wedding cake and a bridal bouquet of dried flowers, along with my white shirt, red bow tie and cummerbund—and all the treats—are either on the disappearing plane or at Air Tindi's loading dock, 310 air miles away.

"Both of us are door knobs. We deserve each another," cries Susie. Then, with great theatrical flair, she screams: "I can't get married without my dress and cake! We'll have to wait till next year and get married on the Thelon. I won't be married without my dress. I won't. I won't. I won't!"

Charging grizzly, foot-stomping musk ox, whirlpool rapid. Nothing can match the fury of a frustrated woman on the tundra. Ultimately, Susie comes to her senses, apologizes and politely informs everyone that she must sulk for three days. We try to pacify her by offering to construct a dress from white plastic poly bags. "You can use my head net for a veil," someone offers weakly.

Fortunately, the rain, the rapids, the beauty of the tundra and the intense physical punishment of the portages encourage perspective and when, at eight that night, camp is pitched, the loss has become a numbing but distant reality.

Sheltered under the multi-colored fourteen-foot tarp, I prepare hot-buttered rum and oriental stir-fry while the crew administers to other chores. The blowtorch whirr of the two cookstoves obscures the hollow sound of distant engines.

"Twin Otter comin' in," yells someone. Sure enough it is a twin—flaps down and a wing dropped; he's circling. Richly emblazoned on the plane's side is the Air Tindi logo. I stop the stir-fry and grab the small, hand-held radio: "Air Tindi Twin Otter, Air Tindi Twin Otter, this is the Cliff Jacobson party. Can you take a message to base for us? Over."

There is no answer. Instead, the plane zooms in and drops to what, from our perspective, is crash altitude. It banks slightly and the co-pilot kicks something out of the door. It is the pack—the white wedding pack! With flair and precision, the twin climbs skyward and wig-waggles a fond goodbye.

Considering the fall, the pack and its contents are in surprisingly good shape. There's a small tear in the bag's double canvas bottom and wide cracks in the plastic containers that hold the pudding cake and frosting. Susie's dress, flowers and accouterments are intact. Everyone cheers as I pour a round of Pusser's rum and toast Air Tindi!

(After the trip, I learn the story from dispatcher Gawletz: "A pilot said there was a white pack on the dock that had a Duluth Tent logo and "Cliff" written on the flap. It was so light I figured it contained town clothes, but when I opened it, I discovered a wedding cake and dress. I knew you guys wouldn't rest till you got that pack, so I put it aboard a northbound twin and asked the pilot to drop it off on the way home. Woulda been nice if we could've found some open water to land, but the guys have kicked stuff out the side door before.")

How's that for going the extra air mile?

For the next ten days, we bask in the joys of the river. There are rapids to run and caribou and musk ox to photograph, and an interesting bear encounter.

Two men were obliviously fishing from their canoe, which had grounded on a small sandbar, when the grizzly came toward them. Curious about the intruders, the bear loped easily at them, coming to an abrupt halt just two canoe lengths away. Momentarily, men and beast stood frozen as they faced one another. Then, suddenly, the bruin turned and galloped full speed away as fast as his powerful legs could carry him. Regrettably, the men in the canoe were too consumed by other thoughts to take pictures.

Three bends south of Wilberforce Falls we came upon an inoperative mine occupied by two Canadian geologists, whom we invited to attend the wedding. It wasbarely three miles from the mine to Wilberforce, so the men enthusiastically agreed to come.

Wilberforce Falls: Bold, impelling, spectacular. Highlight of the north, it drops 160 feet in two successive pitches. By comparison, Niagara Falls drops 167 feet. It has been a dry summer and the water level is very low. Indeed, the west channel—normally a thundering cascade—has been reduced to a picturesque dry column of balconies and caves. The view from the top is breathtaking. To the east, west and south are hundreds of miles of uninhabited tundra. To the north is a water-carved river valley of immense proportions, and the Arctic Ocean. A spiritual place, Wilberforce Falls is a perfect wedding site.

"Better come here, Cliff. Got a rare archeological find," calls a voice excitedly. Sure enough, in a sun-parched cove, its eight legs weighted firmly with smooth stones, is a partially inflated green plastic octopus. Nearby is a note and poem that expresses the good wishes of a Canadian group which passed by three weeks ago. "Ollie" the octopus is now our official mascot and will be an honored guest at the wedding.

The wedding day—August 12, 2 P.M. sharp: Unbeknownst to Sue and I, the crew has prepared a wedding extravaganza. Bridesmaid Brad Bjorklund has scoped out a cathedral-like ceremonial site (which he calls "the chapel of the blue dome") at the upper falls where Susie can be hidden from view until the wedding march announces her grand appearance. Clad in a flowing black robe, marriage commissioner Charlie LeFevere, or "His Excellency," as he came to be known, solemnly approaches the tripod of canoe paddles that serves as the marriage pulpit. Seconds later I appear, clad in newly washed wool trousers, white shirt, red bow tie and cummerbund, L.L. Bean hunting shoes, and a clean white hat. At least one person notices that I have shaved for the occasion. Another questions the "real purpose" of the sheathed knife on my belt.

On my right, nervously clutching the ring—a brilliant green chrome tourmaline set in a rich gold setting—is best man Biff Kummer. Trip physician and philosopher Jerry Noller has provided the guests with formal attire—tuxedo T-shirts.

In unison, the witnesses stand and face the pulpit. One man opens a tiny music box that plays *Here Comes the Bride.* Escorted by bridesmaid Brad, Susie, carrying a mixed bouquet of Wisconsin dried blooms and fresh tundra flowers, steps forward in time with the music. She wears an ermine-trimmed full-length satin dress with flowing train and Green Wellie rubber boots. Bright red lipstick and gentle eye-shadow on her radiant face complete the picture. By any account, she is beautiful. It is 73°, there is a slight breeze, and there are no bugs!

Just before the vows are made, we witness a powerful omen. A huge raven, jet black and preened, flies into the cathedral and perches on a flat rock a dozen feet away. Proud and unafraid, the bird stands and watches. As the ceremony begins, the raven flies away and seconds later, a white gull takes his spot. Everyone— even those who are not religious—is touched by this favorable omen, which Dr. Noller says is "extremely powerful medicine." Later, Jerry reads about ravens from an Indian spirit book entitled *Medicine Cards,* by Jamie Sams and David Carson:

"Raven is the messenger that carries all energy flows of ceremonial magic between the ceremony itself and the intended destination . . . It is the power of the unknown at work, and something special is about to happen. Raven magic is a powerful medicine that can give you the courage to enter the darkness of the void, which is the home of all that is not yet in form . . . Great Spirit lives inside the void . . . Raven is the messenger of the void (and the raven's black color is the color of the void)."

For me, the meaning is brilliantly clear: Sharon had come to tell me that what was about to happen was good and right. In a final act of love, she unselfishly gave her blessing.

Charlie reads the script we have prepared and we end the ceremony with the traditional kiss, after which bridesmaid Brad leads us to the reception site. Spread on a silver space blanket within yards of the thundering falls are all manner of delicacies—smoked oysters, kippered herring, pepperoni and sardines, mixed nuts, mellow mints and rich chocolate bars. The centerpiece of the feast is a white, richly frosted, two-layer pudding cake with a plastic wedding couple on top. Here, near the top of the world, in this land of little sticks, it is all quite unbelievable.

As I pour the wedding cognac, the two geologists stroll forward with a large box wrapped in newspaper and bound with orange surveying ribbon. "All we could come up with on such short notice," says the elder man, who also produces a bottle of 151-proof rum with which to "spike the cognac."

Susie tears open the box and unbelievingly stares at its contents. "It's a toaster, a real toaster!" she exclaims. Sure enough, it is a toaster, and a four-slice model to boot. "Honest, we can really use it," I mumble as I walk my new wife to the pinnacle of the falls for a photograph. As the picture is snapped, a stark white Twin Otter, bearing the words Air Tindi on its side, zooms in from nowhere and buzzes the falls, clearing the upper ledge by a matter of yards. The plane climbs powerfully upward, circles broadly, then wags a salute and turns toward Yellowknife. Later, I learn it was my friend Bob Dannert, enroute home from a trip down the Simpson River.

"I could see it all," said Bob later. "The white dress, red cummerbund and gourmet layout. By the way, was that really a toaster?"

Our marriage was registered in Yellowknife, Northwest Territories, Canada, on August 18, 1992. We live in a restored, 19th-century Victorian farmhouse just outside of River Falls, Wisconsin. Susie teaches Home Economics/Quest to seventh- and eighth-graders at nearby Meyer Middle School. It's a 17-minute drive to Hastings, Minnesota, where I have taught environmental science at the local middle school since 1971. Each summer, Susie accompanies me on my two Science Museum of Minnesota-sponsored canoe trips. Between times, we explore wild places together, on foot and in our solo canoes.

Oh, The Bride She Looked So Sweet Behind A Veil Soaked In Deet

Following the wedding ceremony, Charlie LeFevere, our marriage commissioner, surprised us with a poem he had written during the canoe trip. Susie and I think it captures the essence of the experience.

Sue Harings and Cliff Jacobson
found they shared a love
For wild lands and running streams
and open skies above...

And hoards of flies and Yukon Jack
and soggy woolen coats,
And ice cold baths and blistered feet
and pointy-ended boats.

Now Susie loved adventuring
as much as any lass,
And as she walked, a bowie knife
bounced gaily on her . . . hip.

Cliff, a tundra-tripping guide,
a man of great repute,
A northland Woody Allen
in a red wool union suit.

So when they knew the time had come
that wedded they should be,
It had to be at the River Hood
by the shores of the Arctic Sea.

So, they drifted down the river,
firmly set upon their course,
With eight other bold adventurers
for the falls called Wilberforce.

For solitude they came, then, to this
strange and distant region.
Instead, they found a bunch of chatty,
smiling green Norwegians.[1]

The second day they dined in sun
on Smucker's and ricotta
And sailed on 'fore southern winds—
the Hood River Regatta.

The third day out it rained and rained
and rained and rained and rained
And rained and rained and rained and rained
and rained and rained and rained.

Where they went there were no portages,
no tracks, or trail, or roads,
So they staggered o'er the tussocks
under Herculean loads.

Cliff pushed them on relentlessly—
a heartless, driven meanie.
"Get up!" "Keep moving!" "To the falls!"
and "Don't be such a weenie!"

Past wolverines so treacherous,
lands roamed by hungry bears,
And wolves which stalked them o'er the hills
and vicious arctic hares.

The sky above their only roof,
this wasteland their abode;
They had to squat on barren earth
without e'en a commode.

Their mettle was sore tested
in the stormy tumbling foam.
Boats plunged and dove through freezing drops
and sailed o'er boiling domes.

---

1. We were surprised to encounter six friendly Norwegians in fabric-covered folding canoes. Their trip was sponsored by Helly Hanson, Inc. Every bit of their equipment—from rain suits and packs to nylon splash covers—was forest green in color. There was not a stripe of contrasting color anywhere. It was a rather comical sight.

As they crashed through raging waters,
their canoes were tossed like corks,
And they pulled their hats down o'er their ears
and screamed . . . the sorry dorks.

At last they came to Wilberforce.
The goal they sought was won;
And they stood in awe and wonder
at what nature here had done.

For the river leapt from sunny vales
to deep and frigid caves,
And roared so loud it shook the earth,
and mist rolled off in waves.

The bride was simply stunning
in her gown all fringed in ermine.
The groom looked pretty good himself—
bow tie from PeeWee Herman.

A cummerbund of crimson wrapped
around Cliff's muscled belly.
Sue's dainty feet were clad all 'round
in olive-colored Wellies.

A sic sic and a falcon and a pair
of musk ox cows
Looked on in rapt attention as they
said their wedding vows.

They pledged to stay together on
the river that is life;
And the magistrate joined up their hands—
pronounced them man and wife.

They blithely strolled back to their tent,
afloat on wedded bliss;
And the party heard a giggle
and a big wet juicy kiss.

But now it's time to close the veil—
to leave unheard, unseen,
The smiles, the sighs, the gentle swish
of wool on capilene.

Autumn Magic

Sunrise on a crisp October morning. Anxious hands, chilled by the day's beginning, slip the trim light canoe into the cool green water. Only the muffled chirp of a curious squirrel testifies to the day's awakening. Today, you will put aside household chores and the responsibilities of matching income to expenses, and experience the magic of a free-flowing river. The world, with its attendant troubles, will have to wait till sunset, when the spell will be broken.

You wade the canoe into the determined current, then gingerly climb aboard. Clad in ageless tennis shoes, your feet are momentarily numbed by the cold water. Later, when the sun is high, you'll wring your wool socks and dry them on the thwarts. Already, the day is warming rapidly—perhaps by noon a nap on a sun-warmed knoll will highlight what is already a perfect day.

Round the bend, the river quickens and a mid-stream deadfall calls your paddle skills into play. A gentle stern pry sets the proper ferry angle. You whisper, "Backpaddle," to your partner, and the well-mannered canoe glides obediently out of harm's way. Despite the textbook-perfect maneuver, you are embarrassed that your hushed command has broken the awesome silence of the day.

Beyond the swift, the river broadens. Only the gentle bending of the bottom grasses suggests the direction of flow. Now, you laze back in the canoe and drop your arms to your sides, hands immersed wrist-deep in the cool clear water. Every muscle relaxes as your body attunes to nature. Overhead, a lone cottony cloud punctuates an ocean of azure. Here, there are no schedules or deadlines to meet, no intellectual discussions or arguments. There is just the magic of the river.

Ultimately, you are awakened by the hushed enthusiasm of your partner. "There, there!" she whispers, pointing to a young deer, one-hundred feet away. "Freeze: just float," you quietly command. Dappled in the morning sunlight, the curious fawn stares peacefully your way. You pass within a canoe-length of her tawny body.

It is noon and the high golden sun has flooded the day with warmth and light. High on the heavily wooded hills, the hardwoods are in full color. Golden oaks and rust-red maples blend with summer greens in a palate of vibrant hues. Amidst the flood of luscious colors, a low swooping red-tailed hawk emits a shrill *keeow.*

Canoeing for the Big One

A T THE OUTSET, it should be made perfectly clear that I have no serious interest in fishing. Sure, I like fresh-caught batter-fried walleye as well as the next guy, but I have no patience for the rigamarole of baiting hooks and unsnagging lures. On the rare occasions I do fish, I seldom catch anything. So it came as quite a surprise— even to me—when I agreed to join five friends for a week of "canoe fishing" on a remote river in the heart of northern Canada.

Lagoon-blue water, champagne clear. No sign of humans anywhere. Only the occasional shriek of an eagle breaks the crisp silence of the day. The mist green Old Town canoe slips determinedly into the cool, quiet water of the eddy and two men begin to fish.

In the bow, a muscular boy of sixteen casts a red-and-white Dardevle into a promising backwater where just yards away his dad's lure—a soft-bodied jig baited with belly-meat tail—has already found home.

"Can't hold him," calls Doc, the man in the stern. "Jack, swing us left. Quick! He's goin' under the boat."

Obediently, the boy reaches for his paddle as his dad continues to reel the pike in. Just then, the huge pike turns 180 degrees and begins to run, dragging the canoe behind. Amidst the squealing drag, Jack emits a piercing, "Yeeow!" Another giant pike is on his line and running too.

Envious and amused, we watch the scene unfold: Both fish have chosen the same escape route and they are pulling the canoe sideways at what appears to be phenomenal speed. The two men lean hard left to maintain balance as the craft skids along. Each cranks furiously as the line plays out, but neither accomplishes much.

The fight continues for maybe ten minutes, then the exhausted fish are brought alongside. The fishermen have no nets or gaffs, just bare hands. George and I paddle close to help with the landing. I grab Doc's pole, while George and Jack struggle with the other yard-long played-out northern. Seconds later, the fish is aboard. Jack fumbles for the stringer while Doc and I see to landing its slightly smaller mate. Without a net it's a tricky proposition: This guy's mouth could take my whole hand! Ultimately, it too is aboard and we stare unbelievingly at the two giants, which consume nearly half the length of the canoe.

We estimate the weight of the bigger fish at twenty pounds. The canoe is too tippy to weigh him immediately. We'll do that on land, then let him go. We're after "eating" fish, you understand.

Doc and Jack spin the canoe about and proudly head for shore. They are met by Walt and Harry who had paddled full speed across the bay to see the action. Beaming, Harry hoists a shimmering six-fish stringer—four northerns and two walleyes, thirty-five pounds in all. "Lost a monster," sulks Harry. "Must've gone twenty pounds."

"Sure," says Doc, nonchalantly pointing to the two "little ones" wriggling on the canoe's bottom.

Stunned, Harry and Walt utter forced praise, then, like whipped dogs, paddle silently ashore. In the distance we hear the mutterings of their jealousy.

The seeds of the 1986 trip were planted when Harry and company asked me to suggest a river that offered awesome fishing for big jacks (northern pike) and grayling, complete isolation from other fishermen, a minimum of back-breaking portages and plenty of challenging but non-intimidating rapids.

"How's about the Cree?" I volunteered. "Bob Dannert did it in 1985. He says it's got some of the best fishing on the continent— that northerns over ten pounds are the rule, not the exception. Says it tops even the Hood and Coppermine (tundra rivers in the Northwest Territories) for trophy fish."

At this, Harry launched into a technical dissertation on the essentials needed to catch the "big ones"—all of which might, if carefully packed, fit into a giant tackle box.

"Forget the heavy artillery, Harry, we ain't mad at 'em," said Doc. "What's the river like, Cliff? I'm goin' for the canoeing as well as the fishing."

"Looks interesting," I responded. "She drops about ten feet per mile in the first fifty miles. Should be quite a ride. No lakes, no falls, no people . . . and no portages!"

At this, a hush fell over the group. That was the clincher. A week-long canoe trip without portages on an isolated Canadian river was a nearly unheard-of prize.

"Why, we can just float her and fish," beamed Harry.

"Hardly," I admonished. "This river's a mass of rapids. You guys better learn how to paddle, or you'll be walking out!" With this, I served beer and popcorn and laid into the details.

The Cree River begins at Cree Lake in the remote northwest corner of Saskatchewan. It flows at furious speed about one-hundred and fifty miles north through sandstone bedrock to Black Lake, just east of famed Lake Athabasca. The total drop is 656 feet, most of which occurs in the first eighty-five miles. While there are no dangerous falls or ledges along the route, the steep gradient produces enough hair-raising white water to keep intermediate white-water paddlers on their toes.

The route was first explored by J.B. Tyrrell in 1896, and he suggests the upper river is a mass of nearly unpaddleable white water. For example, he wrote in his *Notes On Two Routes Travelled Between the Churchill and Saskatchewan Rivers:*

"Six miles below (Cree Lake) we reached the head of a long rapid, known as Hawk Rapid, in which the river has a total descent of from thirty to forty feet in a distance of about two miles. (Actually, maps indicate a sixty- to eighty-foot drop) . . . Half-a-mile further down, the river rushes in a wild torrent between abrupt walls of sandstone ten feet in height . . . The rapid is a long and bad one, without any channel. It cannot be tracked with a line and wading in the water is very difficult . . . Paddling is generally impossible. On this account the Indians rarely ascend this river, our Chippewans telling us that but one man had ascended it in the past seven years."

Our research revealed that only four parties had done the Cree since the time of Tyrrell. Bob Dannert was first in 1985, and his account suggested the river was much less ominous than portrayed. Dannert's notes indicated that the route could be easily covered in ten days by intermediate white water paddlers.

Doc and Jack had been with me on wilderness canoe trips before, so they knew the ropes. But the rest of the crew was green and would have to be trained. Two Saturdays of instruction on a local stream did the trick. After this, all that remained was to pack the food and gear, and to mark off days on the calendar in anticipation of the big event.

Our adventure began one-hundred miles from LaRonge, Saskatchewan, when the trailer hitch broke. The trailer flipped and danced sideways down the road for a quarter-mile before we could stop. Damage included a bent axle and canoe rack, a broken storage box and a trashed-out canoe. My beautiful wood-trimmed Old Town Tripper had been sliced cleanly in half by a steel rack support member.

For awhile, I stood gloomily surveying the remains. No use kidding myself, the trip was over.

Fortunately, my friends were more optimistic. Harry disconnected the Suburban from the mangled trailer and wheeled back to Weyakwin, two kilometers away, where we'd passed a gas station. Perhaps he could find a welder. Meanwhile, the rest of us set about mending the canoe rack with wood splints cut from a nearby log.

Ten minutes later Harry was back, a smile on his face and tailed by an industrial welder with a full shop on his truck. There are maybe fifty of these outfits in Saskatchewan—and Harry just happened to find one gassing up at a nearby service station.

How's that for luck?

Forty-five minutes and forty dollars later, we were on our way. Hopefully, we could rent a canoe in LaRonge, though I was skeptical. With few exceptions, "good" canoes are rare in Canadian bush towns.

In LaRonge, we found our choices were buying a new fiberglass disaster, or renting a beat-up sixteen-foot aluminum model of equally bad breeding. "Let's phone some camps, maybe we can turn up something," suggested George.

One call led to another and another, but no luck. Ultimately, we gave up in disgust and decided to rent a tin boat we'd seen earlier. As we left the phone booth, however, I spied a canoe trailer with the familiar Mad River bunny on its side. There were three canoes aboard, all tricked-out personal boats. I figured there was no harm in talking to whoever owned the canoes, even if they weren't for rent.

"Hi, I'm Cliff Jacobson," I said, thrusting out my hand to the trailer owner. "And we're in a helluva mess. Rolled our trailer and lost a boat. Know any place I can rent a good canoe?"

"Rent? In LaRonge? You gotta be kidding," laughed the man. Then, he introduced himself as Bill Irwin, from Mad River Canoe Company, and without reservation suggested I take his personal canoe—a gorgeous sand-colored seventeen-foot Royalex Explorer, outfitted with yoke, knee pads, splash cover . . . the works. And if that weren't enough, he offered paddles, life vests, anything we needed.

"My pleasure, Cliff," he smiled.

For awhile, I stood dumbfounded in the brilliant sunshine. First, the welder, now the Mad River rep. It was obvious the Great Spirit was lobbying on our behalf.

And the luck kept coming. Bill introduced us to his friend Rick Kolstad, a skilled carpenter who spent the afternoon patching our trailer. The hospitality of the two knew no bounds. I'd just lost $3,000 worth of gear, but I was happy—the trip was a "go" and I'd have a "real" canoe to use on the river.

We left LaRonge at about 5 P.M. and motored up the Key Lake Mine road to Seeger Lake and our waiting float plane. It was a tough haul—two-hundred miles over fist-sized gravel, with no services the entire distance. The final test of our nerves and equipment was the three-mile descent over "sugar sand" to Seeger Lake. Midway down, we got a flat on the Suburban, then observed there was less than a quarter tank of diesel fuel remaining. Suddenly, we were in another predicament.

Harry and I disconnected the trailer and drove out to the mine road with hopes of encountering a truck and advice about fuel and tire repair. We were naturally pessimistic, as we hadn't seen a single vehicle on the drive in.

Once again, the Great Spirit smiled: Within minutes, we encountered a road grader and begged for help. "No problem," smiled the driver. "Got a maintenance shop in the bush about twenty miles back. My boss'll help you."

Sure enough, he did. Despite all the other activity in the shop (there was a forest fire nearby) the man took time to mend our tire and top off our fuel supply. No charge, just a warm grin and a friendly handshake.

It took three trips in a radial-engined Beaver float plane to ferry our six-man crew and three canoes the thirty-five air miles to Cree Lake Lodge, where we spent a luxurious night. I've seen dozens of fishing camps in my Canadian canoe travels, but this operation was exceptional. Perched on a rugged overlook, the view was commanding. On a clear day, we could see the full expanse of the twenty-mile long lake. A massive wooden cross, erected a half-century ago by the resident priest, stood sentry for the rising sun.

That evening, Clarence Biller, owner of the lodge, gave us a guided tour of the old Indian mission and priest's quarters (now a museum), then warmed us up with good food and story after story about the big ones that didn't get away.

Harry, our most avid fisherman, hung on every word.

Biller said he'd fished the headwaters of the Cree, but had never been downriver. "Too fast and rocky for fishing boats. Great canoeing, though, I hear."

Harry asked if it was possible to charter a float plane to the interior of the river and eliminate the need to canoe it. Biller told him there were only a few places to land and that he'd be stuck where he was put. "River's too fast and rocky to paddle upstream. If you want to fish virgin waters, you'll need those canoes!"

At this, Harry began checking his tackle.

After a traditional breakfast of sausage and Red River cereal we loaded our canoes and said goodbye to Biller and staff. A perfect cloudless day saw us across the six-mile expanse of Cree Lake to the headwaters of the awaiting river, where we were greeted by a glass-clear pool of azure.

Was it real? Or had we been unwittingly transported to Hawaii's blue lagoon? For awhile, we just sat there, mesmerized by the compelling beauty.

Once on the river, the game would be northerns, walleye and grayling—no lake trout. Despite our eagerness to flex canoeing muscles, we decided to whip the lake for an hour or two, in hopes of landing a few red-fleshed delicacies. The guys tried a few casts and immediately brought up several nice jackfish—a teaser for what would follow later.

As I said at the onset, I care not a wit for fishing. Nonetheless, I occasionally succumb to peer pressure and opt to wet a line. Fortunately, my friends had brought along plenty of extra rods. With exaggerated boredom, I took one, snapped on a quarter-ounce copper spoon, and nonchalantly tossed the lure into the lake expanse. Immediately, there was a tug. "Fouled up already," I spat. Then, without emotion, I started reeling.

The "snag" materialized into a nice six-pound lake trout, which I brought in easily. Just as I reached down to grab it, a bigger fish struck, engulfing the first halfway to the gills. Astounded, I watched the show: I had two lakers on the same hook!

The little guy was lightly hooked so I knew right off I might lose him. A violent smash of his tail and he was gone—big daddy too. Damn! In proud defiance, I slung out the lure once more. It had barely touched water when . . . another hit. The same six-pounder was on again! Seconds later, I felt another tug. Big daddy had done it again too!

Fifteen minutes later, the tired pair were hauled aboard. I kept the six-pounder and threw big daddy back. Then I kept my mouth shut, fearful the guys might think I liked this sport.

We were all apprehensive about Hawk Rock Rapids, a two-mile stretch of prized white water that comes just nine miles into the trip. Dannert warned us about the drop, said it was the most difficult rapid on the river. But except for two easily avoided ledges and some coordinated whitewater maneuvers, the run was easy. The canoes rub-a-dubbed over the sub-surface rocks with barely a murmur.

We camped by 3 P.M., as became our habit, and hauled out the heavy artillery. Doc and Jack had done a number of Canadian canoe trips and had the gear down pat: Four Dardevle's, four Rapala's, a half dozen soft-bodied jigs, a copper spoon, and a few assorted Mepps. They had one extra rod and reel between them. Long experience in the Canadian bush had taught us that virgin-water fish usually bite on anything thrown at them. A cigar box-sized assortment of lures is plenty for a week in the Saskatchewan wilds.

Walt and Harry were "better prepared." Despite our admonitions, each brought two rods—a medium-action "Ugly Stick," plus a mongo salmon rod for the killer jacks. And both brought a full-sized tackle box filled with everything from four-ounce Dardevles to custom lures whose success was, as Harry put it, "guaranteed."

Thank God there are no portages, I thought.

We feasted that first night—and almost every night thereafter—on slabs of double-fileted jackfish, dipped in "special batter" and tenderly fried till golden brown. Fish weighing less than seven pounds were saved for the pot, the rest were dutifully returned to the river.

In the far north, "catch and release" is a way of life. The rule of thumb is that it takes one to two years to grow a pound of fish, so a twenty-pound northern may in fact be thirty or forty years old! For this reason, nearly all Saskatchewan resorts require the use of barbless hooks, and many impose harvest limits that are more stringent than those set by provincial law.

We went one better on the barbless rule by snipping two of the three treble hooks on each lure. This made fish removal a snap and ensured that the big ones we threw back would live to breed again.

Surprisingly, jigs proved to be the killer bait, both for walleye and northerns of every size. In fact, even our trophy 25-pounder fell victim to a half-ounce soft-bodied jig, dressed with a piece of belly meat (sliced from the first catch) on the tail. Most fishermen from the upper Midwest consider jigs purely walleye bait and would scoff at our using them for northerns. But Saskatchewan anglers told us otherwise. Old beliefs die hard!

Grayling were the only fish that wouldn't take our jigs. Black or light-brown dry flies were the sure killer here, though small Mepps and Dardevles often brought them down. We were able to fish dry flies on our spinning rigs by weighting the line with small split-shot sinkers.

The white water between Cree Lake and Hawk Rapids, which we hit on the first day of the trip was the most productive area for the colorful grayling, the largest of which weighed forty-four ounces.

As every fisherman knows, the rule is lightcolored lures for bright days, dark ones for overcast days. But the Cree often surprised us by working opposite. Once we learned to keep an open mind, there was never a time or place that we couldn't catch fish. In the hot spots—eddies on the inside curves, downstream of islands, and at the base of rapids—three casts per hit were average. Sub-arctic rivers are relatively sterile in terms of food: the fish are usually ravenously hungry!

Medium-action rods with twelve- to fifteen-pound lines were the proven artillery. Harry and Walt kept their heavy-duty salmon rods encased the whole time, professing they'd eventually come in handy. The two lightweight spinning outfits with four-pound test lines were grand for whipping up grayling. But it was the medium-action stuff that brought home the bacon each night.

To save space and weight in the canoes and on the airplanes, we left at home our gaffs, nets, billy clubs, ice chests, tin cans and folding anchors. Instead, each canoe carried a basketball net that could be fashioned into an anchor by weighting it with rocks and tying off the ends. This, a scale, a stringer and a bite-proof glove were our only concessions to extravagance. We relied heavily on eggs, Canadian bacon and freeze-dried foods on those few occasions when we didn't eat fish.

Everyone agreed that a half day of fishing and a half day of canoeing was the perfect mix. It worked out precisely that way on the Cree. We cruised out around 9 A.M. each day and camped by two or three in the afternoon. Serious fishing began about five. We enjoyed twenty hours of daylight in this sub-arctic paradise, so preparing a late-night fish supper was never a problem.

In addition to the fish and the great canoeing, the Cree also was remarkable for its awesome isolation and highly visible wildlife. Once beyond Hawk Rapids, we knew the only way out was downriver. On the upper eighty miles of the route, we saw no evidence of humans—not even a scrap of paper or a fire ring. We drifted quietly by fourteen moose—one so close she splashed us in her proud retreat—as well as two woodland caribou, two huge black timber wolves, a wolverine, two black bear and scores of eagles and hawks. At each encounter, the animals stood their ground, eyes fastened upon us, perplexed at our unrecognizable human forms.

I returned to the Cree River in 1988, to lead a "canoe fishing" trip for the Science Museum of Minnesota. While my crew focused on the big ones that didn't get away, I again reveled the beautiful campsites, often high on eskers, and champagne-clear water, the supreme isolation and the proud, fearless wildlife. I remember the river itself as challenging but not difficult to canoe, pretty but not spectacular. In the late 1980s, a run of bad forest fires destroyed much of the west shoreline, reducing the area to an ugly flatland of little sticks. But I know that regular fires kill insect-infested and diseased trees, restore minerals to the soil and improve habitat for wildlife. In two or three decades, I know the scars will have healed and the majestic spruce-fir forests will dominate again. If I'm still around and able when that day comes, I'd like return to this gentle river for a third and final passage.

Inukshuk

This land of ours
has become habitable
because we came here
and learned how to hunt.
Even so, up here where we live
life is one continuous fight
for food and for clothing
and a struggle against bad hunting
and snow storms and sickness.
But we know our land is not the whole world.

–Inuit Song from the early 1920s

Bobby

The "tree line" is the geographic barrier that separates those who can from those who cannot. Get in trouble on the Arctic tundra and you are completely on your own. If you have a radio, passing aircraft and/or "the satellite" may patch your call on to Bathurst Inlet, Cambridge Bay, Coppermine or points south. If your only link to the "outside" is the swiftness of your feet or the speed of your snowmobile, you must rely on skill and knowledge of the environment to survive. Resourcefulness in the face of adversity is a lesson every northern Eskimo and Indian knows by heart.

It is not uncommon to find parts of snowmobiles, outboard motors and three-wheelers scattered helter-skelter across the tundra, hundreds of miles from the nearest community. Ditto for shotgun shells and empty rifle cartridges. Despite the signs of progress, the Canadian Inuit (Eskimo) still hunts and fishes to survive, albeit now with modern tools and methods.

For example: Instead of building traditional "Inukshuks" (mannequins of hand-laid stone) to scare caribou into the spears of hiding hunters, Eskimos now stalk them openly with scope-sighted .30-06s. Skin kayaks are no longer used for hunting, but they are still built for sale to wealthy tourists from the south. Only a handful of old timers can recall how to build the giant skin "umiaks" (women's boats) which, for thousands of years, served as Arctic river pickup trucks.

Most modern Inuits don't know how to paddle a kayak or umiak, let alone how to build one—and for good reason. There's nothing that a traditional craft can do that state-of-the-art aluminum fishing boats can't do better. But the harshness of Arctic water demands compromises. For example, every Lund and Alumacraft boat carries a complete tool kit, plus a second, identical outboard motor.

Twentieth-century advancements and job opportunities make you wonder why modern Eskimos still choose to live in the "land of little sticks," where amenities consist of radio and satellite TV, and buckets of half-day old Kentucky Fried Chicken flown in on the commuter flight from Yellowknife.

Pierre Berton hinted at the answer when, in 1856, he wrote, "Harsh though it is, no man who has not lived here a lifetime can really understand."

I first heard about Bobby in 1983, while canoeing the Hood River in the Northwest Territories of Canada. In those days, there was a lot of exploratory mining north of 60 (the sixtieth parallel). Bush camps and drill rigs sprang up in every likely spot, and from the skies came the constant drone of float planes to service the rigs. For years following the mining rush, there were jobs galore for anyone who could tolerate uncivilized living.

Just prior to boarding the Twin Otter for the flight to Point Lake and the start of our Hood River canoe trip, Yellowknife base manager Bill Gawletz pointed out a small knoll on our map, just east of Takijaq Lake, which was along our route.

"This here's Kid Creek Camp," he said. "We fly in there twice a month. They've got a radio and a chopper and can get you out if you have trouble. The guys have been holed up there for two months now, so they're probably pretty bushed. Tell 'em I said they should feed you good."

Two weeks of strenuous canoeing and portaging brought us to Kid Creek Camp. Located on a high bare hill, the stark white canvas tents were visible two miles away. Four men waited patiently on shore, eager for the diversion of new conversation. A mining engineer in his fifties appeared to be in command. Nearby was a muscular college kid from Saskatchewan who did the heavy work, a clean-shaven helicopter pilot named Brian, and a bushy, white-haired cook. They said that Bobby, their young Inuit maintenance man and jack-of-all-trades, was gone for the day.

We meandered up to the cook tent where we were treated to wonderful home–cooked food. There were blueberry and pumpkin pies, fresh-baked biscuits with jam and honey, coffee, tea, hot chocolate and candy bars. We offered to pay, but our hosts wouldn't hear of it. What they wanted was news from the south, and for the next two hours we deluged them with it.

Ultimately, the conversation got around to Bobby, who was off in the bush fixing a drill rig. He was touted as the best mechanic in the Territories—a quiet, likeable kid who could fix anything. "We have a lot of fun with Bobby," said the mining engineer. Then he told me this story:

"Bobby's never been south, not even to Yellowknife. He's never even seen a paved road or tree, except on TV. So we got to kiddin' around with him one night—told him that in California the trees are so big you can drive a car right through 'em, and so high that we'd have to string aircraft warning lights on the branches if we flew down there. Then, with a dead straight face, Dave here says there are frogs in those trees the size of husky dogs. 'Giant tree frogs, Bobby! We've all seen 'em. Honest!' "

"Bobby bought the part about the giant frogs but not about the huge trees. And here's a guy who flies around on bush planes and can take a Cat apart with a screwdriver and crescent wrench!"

"Tell 'em about the busted Skidoo," prodded the cook. That story went something like this:

Bobby had two vacation days coming, so he decided to combine these with the weekend and drive his snowmobile 120 miles to Bathurst Inlet to see his girlfriend. "Be back in time for work on Monday," he told the others matter-of-factly.

I hail from Minnesota, snowmobile capitol of the world, and when I told this story to the Polaris snowmobile crowd, they gawked with wonder. Seems no one in their right mind would snowmobile 120 miles across a frozen wasteland without a support party. But the idea didn't bother Bobby at all. He missed his girl-friend. What the hell—if the machine broke down, he could fix it.

The men at Kid Creek Camp knew Bobby carried a very complete repair kit and was highly skilled. So they gave him their blessings and said they'd see him in four days.

Eight A.M. Monday came and went. So did 10 A.M., noon and 3 P.M. The men at Kid Creek were worried. It was 32° below and blowing snow. Worriedly, they looked at one another. Bobby knew the route to Bathurst by heart and he could handle any mechanical problem that might come up. Besides, he'd been born and raised on the barrens and had a wealth of Inuit skills to fall back on. "Hell, he probably stopped and built a snow hut," said one man. It was already too dark to fly, so they couldn't go looking for him if they wanted to. If Bobby didn't make it by noon the next day, they'd call for an airplane.

Midmorning the next day, Bobby nonchalantly tooled in on his snowmobile, as if nothing had happened. He had broken an axle about 40 miles from camp. The snow had been blowing pretty hard, so he had built a windbreak, then set up his canvas tent over the machine, intent on repairing the damage. When he saw he couldn't fix the axle, he hacksawed off a piece of his rifle barrel, threaded it and fit it in place. Bobby said it only took about four hours to get the Skidoo up and running again, but the wind was blowing so hard he decided to stay till it let up.

"Hope you guys weren't too worried about me," he said, with a toothy grin. Then he shuffled his feet and softly told them it was okay if they decided to dock his pay.

A Matter of Principle

IN 1971, I OUTFITTED and guided three wealthy Chicago men—the least affluent of which earned a quarter-million dollars a year—on a five-day canoe trip into the Boundary Waters Canoe Area of Minnesota. I was told to provide the finest food, equipment and hospitality—whatever it took to ensure a good time. In return, I'd be well compensated for my services.

For months I worked on assembling the menu. Supper the first night would consist of Minnesota wild rice and mushrooms and the most expensive twelve-ounce filet mignons I could find. After that, I'd resort to the best dried foods money could buy. I mail ordered freeze-dried pork chops, ice-cream, salisbury steak and hamburger. I carried an assortment of the best cheeses and packed fresh garlic, onions, basil and olive oil. Just wait till these guys sampled my linguini! Each night before supper I'd lay out a small linen tablecloth on which I'd serve brandy in long-stemmed plastic glasses. For dessert, there would be popcorn , fresh-baked pie and hot-buttered rum. The food would be a knockout!

And so would the equipment. I would furnish 54-pound Kevlar canoes, lightweight racing paddles, comfort-styled life vests and commodious Cannondale Aroostook tents. Cost was no object: these guys would have the very best!

As I viewed the mound of high-tech gear before me, there arose a gnawing concern: Not one item in the pile smacked of wood smoke. Perhaps a well-worn canvas pack or two and a round of tin cups would add the proper backwoods ambience to the event. So I meticulously substituted some traditional canvas packs for nylon ones, and replaced all the insulated plastic mugs (except mine) with cups of enameled metal.

Confident that an impeccable outdoor experience lay ahead, I packed the van, picked up the guys at the airport and headed north to the Boundary Waters Canoe Area.

Trouble began at the first portage. In the confusion of teaching my crew how to carry the boats and gear, I inadvertently left my camera sitting on a rock at the canoe landing. An hour later I discovered the loss and regretfully told my companions I would paddle back alone and get the camera while they waited at the next portage, which was just ahead.

"No way, Cliff; you ain't goin' back and we ain't waitin' here," said Barry, authoritatively. "How much was your camera, anyway?"

"Ninety-five bucks."

In a flash, Barry unleashed his billfold, ripped out a crisp one-hundred dollar bill and handed it to me with a grin. "This should cover it," he said. "Now let's get goin'."

Momentarily, I stood there dumbfounded, my eyes transfixed on the C-note. The money be damned: I would not leave my camera behind! Instead, I'd teach this man some "wilderness values."

"Sorry, Barry, your money's no good in the wilderness," I said, and thrust the bill back at him.

Before he could answer, an elderly couple pulled up to the landing in a beautiful wood and canvas Seliga canoe.

"Anybody here lose a camera?" asked the man.

"I did, I did," I rejoiced, aware that I'd just lost my chance to teach Barry an important lesson. Oh well, perhaps I'd have another chance.

Later that day, another opportunity to impart my wilderness ethics presented itself when I suggested we camp for the night. We were eagerly searching the shores of the lake for a vacant spot, but every site was occupied.

I squinted at the map, then regretfully confirmed that all the campsites were taken. We would have to portage into the next lake.

"Wait a minute," said Barry, withdrawing his wallet again. "I've got forty bucks here—that should buy us a campsite."

"Your money is no good in the wilderness. We're going on!" I decreed.

The words were barely out of my mouth when we came upon a spectacular unmarked campsite. Located high on a rocky point, it offered a full view of the five-mile lake. And behold, there was fresh-cut wood and enough level space for both tents.

"Wonder of wonders," I mused. Foiled again!

Around supper-time, the sky darkened with gray clouds. I knew I had only a few minutes to batten down the camp and rig a snug rain tarp. I worked quickly, secure in the belief that these guys would be duly impressed when I served them steak and cocktails before a roaring fire in the midst of a thunderstorm.

The camp secured, I backlogged the fire so it would throw heat into our shelter, put on the teakettle and set about preparing supper on my two gasoline stoves.

"How's about a hot-buttered rum," asked Barry.

"You bet!" I said. "Give me a hand, will you, and pour a double shot of rum into those tin cups. Soon as the water boils, add a spoon of brown sugar, a pat of margarine, a dash of cinnamon and some grated nutmeg. You'll find everything you need in that green bag over there."

"Uh, Cliff, there are only three cups here. Where's yours?"

"Here," I replied, handing him my double-walled insulated plastic mug.

Barry took a long look at the plastic mug, then pointedly asked why everyone but me had to drink from a tin cup.

Taken aback by his blatant disdain for my colorful enamelware, I politely mumbled something about "tradition."

"Tradition, hell," bellowed Barry. "Your cup's better. How's about selling it to me?"

Aha! I thought, suddenly aware that another golden opportunity had just presented itself. I said firmly, "Sorry, Barry, your money is no good in the wilderness!"

At that, Barry reached into his billfold and withdrew some money. "Here, Cliff, will you take five bucks for that cheap plastic cup?"

Grinning proudly, I reiterated my position, "Sorry, Barry, your money is no good in the wilderness!"

Undaunted, Barry pulled out another five and threw it on the ground. "How's about ten?" he asked.

Again, with great delight, I said, "Sorry, Barry, your money is no good in the wilderness!" Then I smugly sipped my drink.

Matching my stubbornness, Barry slapped another five dollar bill on the others. "Fifteen," he said, grinning from ear to ear.

At this, I stopped cooking supper and took a long hard look at the three five-dollar bills before me. Fifteen dollars was, after all, a great deal to pay for a plastic cup that cost me less than a dollar.

"What the hell," I shamelessly announced. "Sold!"

With that, my friend rose up like a gallant knight, and with a mischievous air pronounced, "You know, Cliff, I was prepared to go twenty!"

My Son Is Trying To Kill Me!

WEST OF LAKE NIPIGON, in the rocky shield country of Ontario, there flows a spectacular river called the Kopka. At one point, the river plunges downstream in one of the most magnificent falls within the tree line. Here, at what once was called Mink Bridge Portage, the entire contents of the river spill two-hundred and fifty tumultuous feet in three successive drops, creating one of the most spectacular whitewater areas on the continent. You can stand at the top of a high hill near the first falls and watch the stair-step show in its entirety. As one *voyageur* once commented, "It is the land of the lost."

Getting canoes and gear around the falls requires strength and good balance. At the start, there's a mile-long portage that descends through swamp and the waist-high boulders of a long-abandoned stream. The huge water-polished rocks are so slippery that only agile long-legged folk can negotiate them without falling. I've done the Kopka four times and have adopted the following system, which, so far, has not resulted in any bodily damage.

First, everything is carried to the start of the boulder field, where one or two determined athletes take over. An assistant stands by at each end of the canoe ready to grab anything that comes crashing out. One slip, and a broken leg is certain. Even with help, the route is tortuous and precarious. In rain, it is impossible.

The portage ends at the base of a large rapid, in rushing water and more boulders. Loading gear into the canoe and casting off requires careful placement of feet and help from a friend.

A half mile of paddling brings you to a series of three falls, around which are two more portages. One requires lowering the canoe twenty feet straight down a slick canyon wall. After struggling over more boulders, you must paddle across an intensely

beautiful pool, at the end of which is the final drop. The second portage begins in quiet water well away from the falls. It follows a ridge for a few hundred yards, then ends abruptly at the edge of a broken cliff seventy feet above the river. You can claw your way down to the river but a strong rope is needed to lower your gear. I couldn't imagine anyone coming *up* this portage, even with a rope and team of experienced friends.

I told my crew that once we reached the first drop of Wedding Cake Falls, our isolation would be assured. (These falls have no official name. My wife, Sue Harings, called them Wedding Cake Falls because of their spectacular beauty and because they come in layers.)

Imagine my chagrin when, halfway through the last portage (the one with the seventy-foot drop), I encountered a muscular man in his twenties with a Mad River canoe on his shoulders. A trim gray-haired lady carrying a light pack and two paddles plodded unhappily behind.

Startled by the chance meeting, I jammed my canoe into the crotch of a tree and stepped out to talk. The tired-looking young man grinned weakly and continued speechless down the trail. The elderly woman collapsed on a damp log and coldly pronounced, "My son is trying to kill me!"

She said she was 62 years old, though she didn't look a day over fifty. She had canoed and backpacked the wilderness almost every summer as a child and had passed on her love of wild places to her son and daughter. Together, they had paddled many routes in the Boundary Waters Canoe Area and Quetico. For years, she and her son had talked about paddling a wild Canadian river. In the past, she had planned the trips; this time, it had been his turn.

The man had heard about the wonders of the Kopka and the beauty of its stair-step falls. Neither one had any whitewater experience, so they decided it would be safest to travel upstream. "If we pack light, we'll make it," the son told his mom.

In great detail, the lady told how they had gotten the Kevlar canoe up the steep cliff. "Thank God someone left a rope there," she said. "Maybe I can relax now that the hard part is over."

At this, I told her about the next portage she would encounter, and asked if she had brought any rope of her own. "No, just parachute cord," she answered weakly. Disheartened, I described the final portage, with its bone-breaking boulder field.

Again, she groaned and delivered another round of, "My son is trying to kill me!"

Minutes later, the dark clouds that had covered the sky gave way to a chilling rain that could persist for days.

As I put on my sou'wester hat and waterproof parka, I again warned the woman about the boulders ahead and admonished her not to attempt them in the rain. "Maybe you can crash out a campsite around here and stay until the rain stops," I suggested, knowing full well that the dense vegetation prohibited it.

By now, the man had returned for the behemoth-sized pack that sat along the trail. This, plus a pair of small nylon day packs, comprised the entire kit.

"Got a tarp?" I asked, hopeful they could rig a quick trailside shelter to protect them from the chilling rain.

"Nope. Never use one. Besides, there's no room," said the man. Then I asked if they had an axe and saw, which they'd need to maintain a fire if the rain continued. Again, a firm no.

"I think you'll need a rope to get up the next portage," I said, with hopes of convincing them to abandon the trip and go out with us.

"Got this far without one. We'll make it," said the man.

With this, I shrugged a "whatever," and asked him to tell me about their route. The man, with the help of a map, described a long loop that began at Bukemiga Lake, ran westward to Uneven Lake, then north beyond the Canadian National Railroad tracks and east back to Armstrong. I had done most of the route with husky high school kids ten years earlier and it had taken us eight very strenuous days.

"How long you out for?" I questioned. "Ten days," came the reply. "You gotta be kidding!" I exclaimed. "That's possible only if you're going downstream and know the location of every portage. Took us hours to find the portages here," I said, pointing to the area north and south of Aldrich Lake.

At this, the man smiled courteously, zipped up his parka and plunged confidently ahead. Momentarily, he halted, looked back and called, "Better get going, Mom, before the rain gets worse."

The gray-haired lady struggled reluctantly to her feet, put on her pack, and with proud cynicism, again proclaimed that her son was trying to kill her!

It was a day's paddle from the base of Wedding Cake Falls to the public landing at Bukemiga Lake and our waiting van. As we posed for a final photograph, I told the woman who had shuttled our vehicle about the man and woman we had met on the Kopka. I asked that she share my concern with the charter float plane companies that serviced the area.

Several months later, I received a phone call from a crew member who had seen the woman at a canoe event in Minneapolis. She told him that disaster struck within hours after we parted. Her son had slipped in the boulder field of the first portage and sprained his ankle, which became so swollen he could not walk without the aid of a makeshift crutch. Going back the way they had come was impossible. And so was staying put. Reluctantly, the pair decided to continue, hopeful they would run into a canoeist or fisherman who would help them out. But the remote route they had chosen skirted both casual canoe traffic and the fly-in fishing trade. Their ten days passed, and they saw no one.

Remarkably, the pair made it as far as Aldrich Lake before they collapsed in exhaustion. The man's ankle had swollen to the point where he could not remove his boot. They ran out of food on the twelfth day, and had to rely on fish that, fortunately, were easy to catch. In desperation, they lit a large smoky fire that they hoped would attract an airplane.

In late afternoon on the fourteenth day, they heard the low thumping whir of a deHavilland Beaver. Quickly, they piled green branches on their campfire and said a prayer. Moments later, the plane touched down and rescued them. The woman's daughter had called area police when her mother was overdue, and the police had gotten the plane in the air. However, all the daughter could tell rescuers was that her mom and brother were canoeing upstream on the Kopka. Fortunately this, coupled with the sketchy information I had supplied, had initiated a search of the Aldrich Lake area. Ironically, several aircraft had flown over the couple earlier in the week, but had not seen them. Their blue and green clothing and clear Kevlar canoe had been invisible from the air. It was the smoky fire that had brought down the airplane.

The following spring, I saw the woman at a canoe symposium in Minneapolis. When I asked her if she would ever do another Canadian river with her son, she replied, "No way! He has too much testosterone! Next time I'm going with my daughter. She has estrogen, the gentle hormone."

LeAnn

I MET LeAnn Demars in the summer of 1987 when she and her fiance, Scott Minar, signed up for a canoe trip I was leading for the Science Museum of Minnesota. A petite 30-year-old, LeAnn looked almost too frail to undertake a whitewater adventure that included portaging heavy canoes and equipment over rugged trails. But within her wiry hundred-pound frame was the determination of an athlete and the warm heart of a caring friend.

LeAnn's first love was downhill skiing, which she pursued with gusto. She was also a serious scuba diver. Indeed, the license plate on her compact sedan read CAMAN—a reflection of her dedication to the sport. When LeAnn read about the Fond du Lac River, Saskatchewan, canoe trip in the science museum catalog, she had pestered Scott to sign up, knowing full well that participants must be capable whitewater paddlers. Also aware that she and Scott had much to learn, the pair signed up for my "Basic River Canoeing" class, which I offered through the museum. As I watched them practice on a crisp spring morning, I realized that neither one had the foggiest notion of whitewater procedures. Deep down, I wondered if they'd never make it beyond the first rapid on the Fond du Lac.

Of course, none of my concerns phased LeAnn, who, with an ever-present smile, shrugged off the potential consequences. Indeed, the pretty lady laughed at everything, even when they nearly capsized. When I questioned her about her always-upbeat behavior, she told me that her condition had been diagnosed as "terminal giggles"—sadly, an incurable disorder.

The Fond du Lac is not a difficult river to canoe, but the rapids do require sober attention—a response that was out of the question for LeAnn, who, whooping and hollering, would power straight toward a rock then, by millimeters, miraculously avoid it. One man suggested that her giggles confused the currents. But the rest of us knew it was beginner's luck.

I think it was after supper on the fourth day that Scott confided paddling whitewater with LeAnn, though a very good time, was a life-threatening experience. He asked if they could split up. Nothing permanent, mind you—"Just to teach her how to read rapids," he said.

Next morning, I rearranged the crews and took LeAnn, who, strangely enough, was soberingly quiet. Ordinarily, she was a quick learner who remembered what she was taught. But today, she reacted sluggishly and barely cracked a smile. I wondered why she was suddenly so out of character. Perhaps she and Scott had had a fight.

As soon as we put up camp that night, LeAnn retired to her tent without a word. Scott said she was simply tired. In the morning, I served breakfast—Red River cereal with mixed fruit and brown sugar—on a sun-splashed outcrop above a picturesque falls. Everyone was there but LeAnn, who always was eager to help with camp chores and usually was the first to arrive. Now I was really concerned, for here was a picture-perfect breakfast setting and my new partner was nowhere to be seen.

"Where's LeAnn?" I called, curiously. "Still sleeping," confided Scott, apprehensively. "You guys have a fight or something?" I asked.

"No, I think she's really sick. Threw up last night, says she doesn't want to eat. She can barely sit up."

I consulted with Jim and Cindy Leavitt, a doctor/nurse team from Eau Claire, Wisconsin, who had accompanied me on wilderness canoe trips before. The most probable diagnosis was the flu—hopefully, the short-lived, three-day variety for which rest was the only treatment. I had a supply of broad-spectrum antibiotics that we could try if LeAnn's condition didn't clear up in a day or two. But meantime, serious travel was out of the question.

I looked at my map and date line. We were on schedule and could afford some down time. So I gave the command to "lay over," with hopes that LeAnn's condition would improve by the next day.

LeAnn didn't leave her tent that day. And except for a few sips of instant chicken soup that Scott managed to force down, she ate nothing. Her temperature was 102° and she was feeling worse. At nine the next morning, there was no change in her condition. A light south wind and high clouds suggested prolonged rain was on the way. I had canoed the Fond du Lac twice before and remembered the many long rapids that lay ahead, knowing the rain would make them that much more difficult.

LeAnn's illness had now become a two-edged sword. On the one hand, if we waited another day for her to recover, we would be two days behind schedule and would have to press hard to make our chartered float plane. If the weather deteriorated—which seemed certain—we could lose another day or two, as I would not subject LeAnn to the combined rigors of whitewater and bad weather. Admittedly, I was a skilled paddler and could probably pilot the boat through the bad stuff alone. But soloing a loaded Old Town Tripper with a helpless person aboard was a scary proposition. Better to go now and get the rapids out of the way while the weather was good than to chance them later in a storm.

I discussed the scenarios with the crew, then went to talk with LeAnn, who for nearly two days had eaten nothing.

Courageously, the little lady rolled over in her sleeping bag and propped herself up on one elbow. "I can do it, Cliff," she assured me. "I know we can't hang around here forever."

We took her temperature again. It was 101, down one degree from the day before.

"Okay," I said gently. "Let's paddle."

An hour later, we were on the water and into our first easy rapid. LeAnn tried her best, but she had no strength. Her mind was sluggish and her muscles would not respond. Worst of all, she had no balance and I became fearful we would capsize. Fortunately, there was no wind or rain. The temperature hovered at 66°, and the sun shown brilliantly between the slowly building clouds.

"God, please just get us through these rapids before it rains," I prayed.

By the time we camped, it was obvious LeAnn was too sick to continue, so we formulated a new plan. If, by morning, she was still too sick to travel, we'd rig a bed for her on the bottom of my canoe so she could sleep while I paddled. Jim and Cindy were proficient whitewater paddlers—they would lead me through the rapids. The rest of the boats would follow closely behind, ready to rescue us if necessary. The plan would work fine as long as we were very cautious and the weather remained stable.

Next morning, we bundled LeAnn in layers of fleece and wool

and helped her into my canoe, where minutes later she fell fast asleep. The plan worked perfectly until a cold, chilling rain began. I put ashore immediately and snapped down the canoe's nylon belly cover, which stretched from the bow seat to the stern thwart.

The temperature dropped into the forties and the icy drizzle continued. LeAnn began to shiver and I piled more clothes on her, but they weren't enough. So we stopped paddling, threw up a rain tarp, and built a gigantic fire that blasted flames so hot they fairly vaporized the rain. Minutes later, our shelter was a toasty 85 degrees.

For the better part of the day we drank boiling hot tea and napped in the warmth of the fire, hoping the rain would stop. It didn't. Indeed, the sky suggested the cold drizzle would continue for days. If we stayed much longer, we would miss our airplane; if we pressed on, we jeopardized LeAnn's safety, and possibly our own. To make matters worse, the canoe-length space where we had set up the tarp was the only flat spot around. There was simply no room for tents. If we decided to stay, the entire group would have to rough it under the tarp, a significant portion of which was occupied by LeAnn. What to do? It was a trip leader's nightmare!

At 4 P.M., I reluctantly made the decision to move to a nice camp spot below Brassy Rapids—a narrow, twisting pitch that in good weather is a whopping fine time. But could I pilot the canoe alone through Brassy's many turns and ledges? There was no choice. I would have to.

LeAnn drifted in and out of sleep as we carried her in her sleeping bag to the foam pad on the bottom of my canoe. We covered her with a second sleeping bag then snapped down the nylon splash cover to protect her from the rain.

Momentarily, LeAnn peered out between the folds of insulated nylon and deliriously questioned if she would be safe if we capsized in the rapid. "No problem!" I assured her. "First of all, we won't tip over. And if we do, I'll get you out. Promise!"

I stared at the trusting cargo in the belly of my canoe and said a silent prayer. I wondered, could I really keep my pledge if we tipped over? Vowing to take no chances, I snugged up to the center thwart and numbly pushed off into the mist and foam that defined the start of the three-mile-long, Brassy Rapids.

Immediately, I put the canoe into reverse gear, and kept it there. Brassy was higher than I had expected, with powerful waves, well-defined eddies and confusing channels. A draw to the right, then crossdraw left. Hard back, then ferry right. Through a "vee," follow the slick, over a small drop, turn left hard, then right. There was no time to question the route, only to respond.

Just before the final drop the channel split three ways. The right looked impassable, as did the left. And dead ahead, with barely two feet between them, were two small boulders. Instinctively, I leaned the canoe to the bilge, braced hard on my paddle, and miraculously slid through. An eddy turn around the rock into the slick below, and I was home free. From here, it was simply a matter of picking and choosing my way down the rocky runout at the bottom.

As I floated into the deep quiet water that marked the end of the rapid, I paused to watch the rest of my crew. It was a Laurel-and-Hardy show, as one canoe after another was impaled on rocks. One canoe swamped above the narrow passage I had squeezed through.

Relieved at last from the responsibility of command, I just watched and smiled. LeAnn slept through it all, oblivious to what might have been.

We set up our tents on a beautiful hill at the base of the rapid, then rigged two ten foot rain tarps and built a roaring fire in front of them. An hour later, we heard a shy giggle from beneath the rain tarp. LeAnn's temperature had broken. She was feeling well and ravenously hungry.

I handed her a bowl of thick vegetable noodle soup, which she devoured with an elfish grin. "We paddle any rapids today?" she asked.

LeAnn Demars was killed in an auto accident on August 24, 1990, near Forest Lake, Minnesota. She was 33 years old. The driver of the other car was drunk.

Scott Minar told me that LeAnn regarded the Fond du Lac River canoe trip as the most wonderful experience of her life. I always will remember LeAnn's smile and enthusiasm, and her unwaivering confidence in me. I am proud to have known her and to have shared the wonders of a wild river with her.

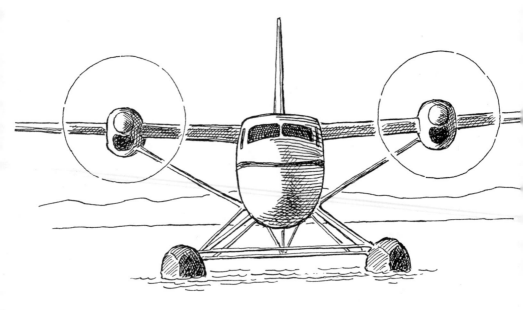

Turbo Sky Horse

WITH A PAYLOAD of three-thousand pounds, full instrumentation and extended range capability, the deHavilland Twin Otter has rightly earned the title, "Workhorse of the North." This 1950s-vintage freight hauler can carry up to twenty-one passengers—or half that number and all their gear—to the most remote regions of the world without need for a groomed runway. Seasonally equipped with wheels, skis, floats or tubby "tundra tires," the Otter can land almost anywhere—on open water, sand beaches, ice or snow, level or bumpy ground, or the scrubby tundra of a high esker. Some planes have both floats and wheels and are truly amphibious, but for big crews with lots of gear, the Twin—especially the faster "turbo Twin"—has no peer. From Africa to Alaska, the deHavilland Otter remains the ultimate sky horse for those who take wild places seriously.

The majority of float-equipped Twin Otters earn their keep by freighting mining equipment, prospectors, fishermen and groceries to northern bush camps and native communities. Occasionally, the planes earn a break from this routine by accomodating hikers and canoeists. One Twin Otter made history when it flew world-renowned Arctic explorer Will Steger's dogs and gear from Minnesota to Antarctica. Another ferried members of England's royal family to a remote arctic river. Everyone who travels the far reaches of the continent eventually comes to love these grand old airplanes and the saucy men and women who fly them.

You don't have to see a Twin to identify it. Miles away, you can hear the high-pitched growl of the turbos. The plane landing on water is a sight to behold. First, the pilot circles the lake several times, one wing dropped so he can check for rocks that might pierce the pontoons. Once the pilot is assured and committed, the plane comes in at what seems to be furious speed. The floats touch water one at a time and the aircraft suddenly slows. At the final approach, the pilot reverses an engine and pivots the craft 180 degrees so it can be backed onto the beach for an easy exit. As the plane rotates, the growl of the engine fades in and out until seconds later, the prop shuts down, and all is mysteriously silent.

Twin Otters are among the most expensive bush planes to fly. As of this writing, charter costs run more than $6 per mile – nearly three times the cost of chartering the popular Cessna 185. This seems exorbitant until you discover that for a crew of six or more, this is the cheapest way to fly, especially if you must carry canoes or bulky gear.

The last deHavilland Twin Otter rolled off the assembly line a few years ago, which makes the plane a collector's item of sorts. But Twins were never cheap—a low-mileage, late-model turbo on floats may go for more than a million dollars, which makes it a very costly curio. For this reason, only the very best pilots fly Twin Otters; the rest bide their time in smaller Cessnas and Beavers until they become multi-engine rated and "ready" for the big sky horse. A few exemplary pilots like Ray X, who flew us home from a Cree River adventure, become instructors. Ray was one of the most skilled and colorful bush pilots I've known.

Ray's chartered Twin settled onto the water like a yellow leaf in autumn. Engine throttled with unnatural ease, it slipped sideways toward us, where it came to rest just inches from the dock. A friendly pot-bellied man in his mid-fifties, Ray came complete with an ever-lit cigarette that he brandished proudly. In a feat of showmanship, Ray slapped a rolled magazine against the inside windshield. "Seven with one blow," he proudly exclaimed as he shook the dead mosquitoes into the lake.

Then, he lit up again and asked, "Where you guys wanna go?"

"Seeger Lake," I said, wondering if he'd checked with the dispatcher before he took off.

"Got a map in here somewhere," he muttered, and began to grope in the cockpit.

Seconds later, he withdrew a half-disintegrated chart that did not include Seeger Lake.

"Got it on your map?" He asked, grinning.

Regrettably, my topo map began well north of our intended destination.

"No matter, I can find it without a map," Ray said. "Near the tote road, ain't it?"

"Yeah," I whispered, hoping he really knew where he was going, and was just pulling my leg.

Without a word, he tapped the fuel gauge and squinted at the needle. "Got just enough gas if we don't screw up," he beamed. Then, he focused in on our three canoes and mound of camping gear.

"Where ya gonna put those three boats?" he questioned.

"In your airplane," I answered.

"Show me."

With that, he perched lazily against the wharf, lit up another cigarette and began a dissertation on how he'd flown Twin Otters for twenty years and never, ever saw anyone put three canoes inside. "One's easy, two'll go. But the only way that third one will fit is if you saw it in half."

Amiable and open-minded, Ray was content to sit on the dock and puff away while we and his co-pilot—a kid of about twenty— did the leg work.

Theoretically, the Twin Otter is a 21-passenger airplane. There are fifteen seats on the right side of the fuselage, and six on the left, near the wide doors. But on most working Twins, the starboard seats have been removed to provide cargo space for bulky equipment. This leaves room for six passengers plus gear. The unorthodox arrangement of Ray's Twin—five seats on the left and one lone seat opposite the emergency door—didn't seem important until the three canoes were nested and stacked tightly against the starboard wall.

I immediately relayed my concern—a frightening lack of space—to the pilot, who was lighting up again.

Ray turned to me with mild curiosity and gazed at the cubbyhole around the solitary seat. "Hell, Cliff, you're a little guy, you can fit in there. Just duck down—it's only a twenty–minute flight."

Weakly, I nodded okay.

Finally, everything was in order and Ray inspected the cargo. As he cinched down the long Herc cargo straps, a canoe shifted and nearly punched out a window.

"Hmmm . . . " said Ray, "You guys use Herc straps on your boats?"

"Nope, not ever."

"Hell with 'em, then!"

This was followed by more profanity when Ray noticed that my seat belt was firmly pinned beneath the seat rail by the weight of three canoes and mounds of camping gear. He scratched his head, then said, "We could unload the airplane . . . Or, Cliff, you could ride without a seat belt. Whatcha think?"

Everyone was getting antsy to be off, so I nodded approval of the second option and climbed aboard. Getting into my perch wasn't easy—I had to crawl through the cockpit onto the right pontoon, then re-enter the airplane through the emergency door by my seat. I would ride, without a seat belt, with my head ducked into the belly of an Old Town Tripper canoe. Oh well, I could endure anything for twenty minutes.

I climbed aboard and slammed the door, which surprisingly refused to lock. "Uh, Ray . . . the door won't stay shut!"

"Don't worry," he replied. "Just hold her tight till we're airborne."

"Yeah . . . okay."

Minutes later, we were cruising down the lake, full throttle, flaps down. Momentarily, I let up my death hold on the door handle and it flew open, spraying water into the airplane. "Jesus Christ," I screamed as I yanked shut the door and hugged the Old Town's thwart with my free hand. I screamed at Ray, but it was too noisy for him to hear. So, I prayed I wouldn't be thrown out of the airplane. Finally, we were aloft, flying south toward Seeger Lake, hopeful we'd find the place before Ray ran out of gas.

Exactly nineteen minutes later, the plane dropped onto Seeger Lake and taxied straight toward our dusty Chevy Suburban. Ray shut down the engine, tapped the gas gauge again and smiled broadly. I gratefully released my death holds on the door handle and canoe thwart.

"Thank God you finally set her down," I called. "I couldn't hold that door shut much longer!"

"I told ya to hold her tight when we took off, Cliff." Ray said. "Hell, there's a ton of force against that door when we're airborne. Good thing you grabbed her when we set down, though!"

Canadian Hospitality

TAKE ONE CANOE TRIP in northern Canada where things go less than butter smooth, and you'll understand the true meaning of "Canadian hospitality." The caring pulse of the northland is especially strong when you get north of the sixtieth parallel.

In 1989, five friends and I paddled the remote Burnside River in the Northwest Territories. Rather than terminate our trip at the Eskimo village of Bathurst Inlet, which is the usual practice for those who canoe this river, we decided to continue along the ocean to the mouth of the Hood River, about thirty miles away. From there, we planned to hike ten miles overland to spectacular Wilberforce Falls, where we would rendezvous with a team of Danish canoeists.

LaRonge Aviation had instructions to pick us up at the mouth of the Hood on August 10. It was August 7 when we arrived at Bathurst Inlet. Ten hours of calm weather and a bit of luck would see us to the Hood River and the base of the towering Wilberforce hills.

There was a lot of activity in the hamlet of Bathurst Inlet on the day we arrived. All the school-age children—about two-thirds of the village's twenty-five inhabitants—were making ready to board the "school bus" (a Single Otter on floats) for the ride to Cambridge Bay and the new school year. It was a somber time for the parents, who would not see their kids till Christmas. The youngsters, however, were excited about making new friends and seeing a real town that had movies, television and foods (like pizza) they'd heard of but never tried.

I struck up a conversation with the float plane pilot and learned that a huge rough weather system was expected within twenty-four hours. "Better fly out now while you can," he advised. The alternative was to beat it down the coast to the mouth of the Hood, and

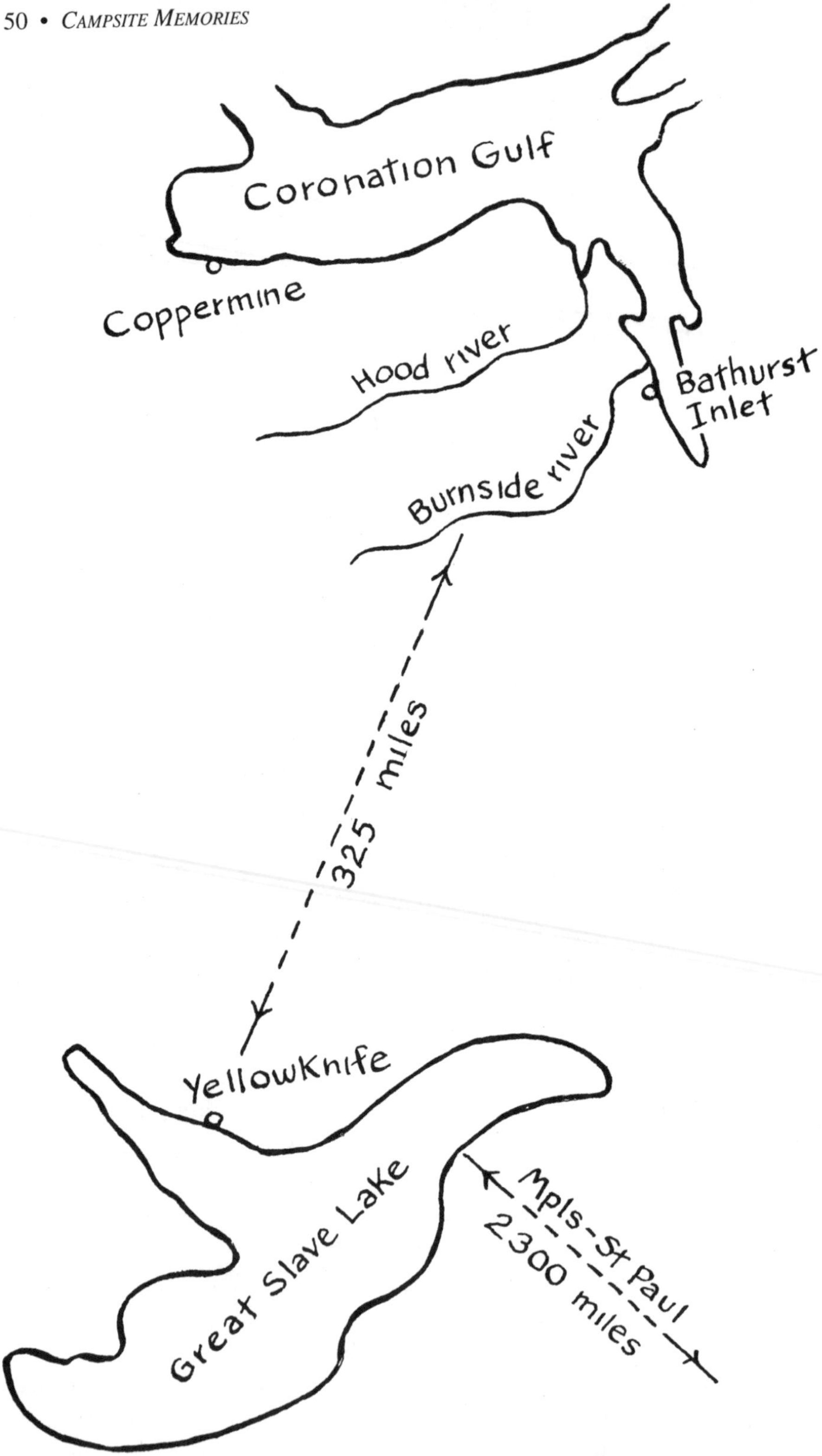

Coronation Gulf

Coppermine

Hood river

Bathurst Inlet

Burnside river

325 miles

YellowKnife

Great Slave Lake

Mpls-St Paul
2300 miles

maybe get socked in there—or somewhere along the way. Hmmm
. . . this called for a group decision. Laying there in the warm sunshine amidst a bustle of human activity provided the impetus we
needed to abort the ocean traverse and fly out before the storm.
Bathurst Inlet Lodge, though closed for the season, had a radio,
and we were welcome to use it to call LaRonge Air and request a
pickup. I asked the dispatcher to call LaRonge and check on our
Twin Otter.

"Call you back in an hour," he promised.

He did, delivering the message that the LaRonge Twin was
booked and couldn't pick us up till the appointed time. "Want me
to line you up a Twin from another company?" he asked.

"Yeah, but first get me a price."

An hour later, the radio clicked on again with the words that
Rae Calm Air had a Twin on floats ready to go immediately. Price
was $3,418 Canadian—$200 more than the return fare agreed to
by LaRonge Aviation. Did I want it?

"You bet!"—It was unanimous—except for one dissenter who
argued we'd have to forfeit the $3,218 we paid in advance to
LaRonge for the promised return flight. He felt LaRonge wouldn't
return the deposit, which was locked in the company safe.

I tried to convince him that we were dealing with a bush plane
operation, not commercial jet service to New York. But no deal.
After an hour's bickering, I gave up and agreed to pay the three
grand myself, if it came to that—though I knew, of course, it
wouldn't.

The chartered Otter came on schedule and we arrived in
Yellowknife in the wee hours of the morning. First stop—
LaRonge Aviation to get our deposit for the return flight. Flight
dispatcher Bill Gawletz (who now works for Air Tindi) met us
with a grin and an outstretched hand, along with apologies for not
coming to get us.

Smiling, Bill returned the envelope of money and asked what
the other air carrier had charged us for the flight out. Then, he
began pushing buttons on his calculator.

"Whatcha doin' Bill, giving us a discount on next year's trip?"
I asked.

"Hmmm . . . $5.37 a mile; that's fair." Bill said. "We charged
you $5.12—last year's rate. Just checkin' to make sure you guys
weren't ripped off." Then, he began an emotional dissertation on
how canoeists take nothing from the land and leave nothing

behind. We haul out the trash others bring in, and we don't stand around with our hands in our pockets and watch his pilots load the aircraft. We respect his planes and the men who fly them.

"Most of my customers have no affinity for the land, no love for it. To them, we're just sky taxis. But you guys are special. You respect the environment and my operation. I don't want anyone messing over my canoeists!"

Throughout the Canadian northland there are caring people like Bill Gawletz, who earn a living from the land yet are sensitive to its pulse and appreciative of those who paddle canoes and share the dream that wilderness can, with effort, be preserved.

The American wilderness canoeist may not be a noble species, or even an endangered one. But on the whole, he treads lightly and treats wild places with knowledgeable concern. Certainly, there are outlaws in the ranks, and they earn the harshest disdain. Nonetheless, most experienced backcountry paddlers I know deserve the generous Canadian respect. Though American travelers have no political clout in Canada and no rights other than those granted by the Canadian government, they should continue to treat the land honorably. For myself, that's a promise!

It was 5 A.M. when we taxied into Yellowknife harbor. Rae Calm Air was not yet open for business, so the pilot suggested we stop back later to pay our bill. After a hearty breakfast of ham and eggs at the famed Wildcat Cafe, we casually loaded our trailer, then drove to the Rae Calm float base. It was 9 A.M. and there was considerable confusion. The radio was barking and the dispatcher was engrossed in putting a location pin on the flight board.

"Hi, I believe I owe you some money," I yelled over the roar of a churning propeller. "Oh, you must be the Cliff Jacobson party," the dispatcher replied. "Let's see now, that's $3,418, right?"

"You guys are awfully trusting. We coulda blown this place hours ago without paying our bill."

"Nyah, canoeists are wonderfully honest; they always pay their bills," she smiled.

Beer and Medicine

IF YOU WANT SPECTACULAR SCENERY, challenging rapids and great fishing, canoe the Pipestone River from north of Pickle Lake, Ontario, to the Winisk River, and on into Hudson's Bay.

My friend, Dr. Tom Schwinghamer did just that in 1989. Tom's paddling companion, George Loban shared this story with me:

"It was God-awful hot. For days, my pocket thermometer registered 100° in the shade. In the sun, the mercury was off the scale. Not even a breeze to ripple the water. It was calm. Dead calm. And like I said, God-awful hot. We changed our routine and began paddling at sunrise when it was relatively cool (80°). By ten, it would be 90°, 100° by noon. We'd rig a shade tarp for lunch, have a swim, drink some Kool-Aid, have another swim, drink some more Kool-Aid and have another swim. On the third day, heat monotony set in and we renamed the Pipestone the Gobi River. We carried around 'Desert Falls' and lined 'Heat Stroke Ledge.' We nearly died horsing our canoes between the trees on 'Refried Brains Portage.' Each night, we'd all face west and reverently pray for rain!

"By mid-afternoon on the fourth day, the temperature hit a record high of 103°. 'Give anything for a cold beer,' muttered Tom, sweat pouring down his face. 'How much is anything?' I asked.

"'Look there,' said Tom. 'A dock, ain't it?' Sure enough, it was. And sitting dolefully on the end of it was a huge, pot-bellied man with his head in his hands and his eyes hypnotically fixed upon the water. 'Looks like the guy's sick,' I said. 'Nyah, fat Phil probably had too much beer and dropped his wallet in the lake. Let's sneak up on him,' whispered Tom.

"So using our quiet Indian underwater stroke, we paddled right up to the dock without him noticing us at all.

" 'Boo!' yelled Tom, and the guy damn near leapt into the drink. Then he jumped up, and like a broken record repeated, 'Any of you guys a doctor? Any of you guys a doctor?'

" 'That depends on how much beer ya got!' said Tom dryly.

" 'Quick, Doc, quick, you gotta help my friend. He's got diabetes and he keeps falling asleep. Plane won't come till Thursday (it was Monday). I think he's gonna die.'

" 'Okay, relax,' said Schwing. 'Let's have a look at your friend.'

"Tom and the rest of us followed the man—who we continued to call Phil even after he told us his real name was Bill—into the tiny fishing cabin. There, speechless and half-awake, was his friend.

" 'Got any sugar?' asked Tom.

" 'No.'

" 'Maple syrup or Karo?'

" 'Yeah.'

" 'Get it and start feedin' him some,' ordered Tom. 'Don't stop till he says he wants to drink beer again.'

" 'Okay,' said Phil . . . I mean Bill.

"Minutes later, the sick guy came to and told us his name was Brian, and that he and buddy Bill flew in for a few days of fishing. 'I shoulda told Bill to feed me sugar if this happened,' said Brian. Then, with grand gestures, he thanked Doc Schwinghamer for saving his life and asked how he could show his gratitude.

" 'Got any cold beer?' smiled Schwing.

" 'You bet,' said Brian, and he ordered Phil . . . er, Bill . . . to get Doc one. Bill pulled a cold LaBatt's Blue from the cooler and handed it to Tom, who instantly whipped off the cap and downed the contents in a single swig. Meantime, the rest of us looked on wishfully.

" 'How's about another beer?' asked Tom, hopefully. 'Sure, sure Doc,' said Bill, and he handed Doc another Blue, which Tom worked on steadily for the better part of a minute.

" 'Got one for my buddies?' asked Tom.

" 'Hmmm, gee, I dunno,' said Bill. 'We only got half a case left and we got three more days here.'

"At that, Brian rose from the cot like a ghost from the grave, and in a half-rage bellowed, 'Jeezzus Christ man, the guy just saved my life and all you can give him is two measly beers. Hell, man, give him all the beer!'

"After that, all I remember is the six of us downing the remaining twelve bottles right on the dock, and we didn't even offer one to Phil. I mean Bill!"

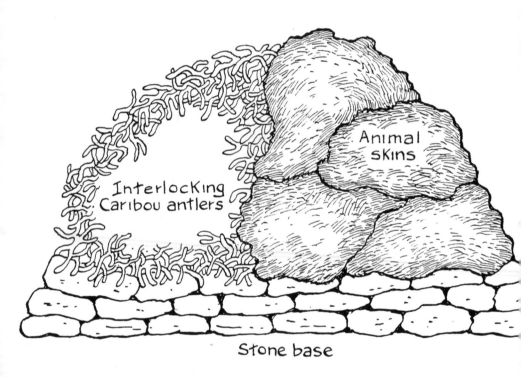

Animal skins

Interlocking Caribou antlers

Stone base

Nadlak

FLOWING THROUGH THE TUNDRA of the central Canadian arctic is the remote, powerful Burnside River. With an average drop of more than 15 feet per mile and an average July flow of 17,200 cubic feet per second (compared to 4,850 for Canada's Coppermine River), the Burnside commands respect. From its start at Contwoyto Lake, just below the Arctic Circle, to its triumphant finish at Bathurst Inlet on the Arctic Ocean, rapids abound continuously, worsening as you approach the sea.

The Burnside flows through rugged hills that rise to fourteen-hundred feet, creating an ominous feeling that you're in the "land of the lost." The last fifty miles are characterised by scenic views so breathtaking you can barely "keep your eyes on the road." To this, add frequent sightings of musk ox, caribou and grizzly bear, plus some of the finest fishing in the world, and you can see why the Burnside was high on my list of rivers to paddle.

My journal entry for August 1, 1988, reads:

"Water levels in the Territories are the highest ever recorded. There was standing water in the ditches along the Mackenzie Highway on the drive up—unheard of in late July. Locals told us the road to Fort Smith had just re-opened; it had been completely washed out a few weeks ago!

"I would not have expected the rain to have affected us this far north. But the rapids on the river just keep getting bigger and bigger. Every tundra creek has water and it's all pouring into the Burnside. The first eighty miles are best described as one continuous rapid! Glad we have our nylon splash covers. I can't imagine doing this river without them, or our wonderful Old Town Tripper canoes.

"Three-thirty P.M. I am sitting right now on the stone foundation of what appears to be an ancient Inuit dwelling. The floor of the hut is constructed of table flat stones (where on earth did they find them?) and the walls are built from caribou antlers—thousands of them, maybe tens of thousands! There are fifteen huts on this island, which is no bigger than a football field. Five of the huts are constructed from antlers, the rest have low stone walls. Why the difference? A wooden stake and some orange surveying ribbon suggest this is an archaeological site. What a rare find! And in the middle of nowhere. My guess is that this is an old Inuit caribou hunting camp. But why so far (two-hundred miles) inland?

"The place looks like maybe ten families (forty people?) could have lived here year-round. How on earth could they maintain sanity and privacy? The island is maybe 100 yards long and two-thirds as wide. And not a tree, hill or boulder in sight. The huts are very small, barely twelve feet across, hardly enough room for a growing family.

"The water around the island is very shallow, an ideal spot for caribou to cross the river. I can just see the Inuit spearing them from their kayaks. The place must have been a real meat market. In summer, the Eskimos probably kayaked to the mainland. In winter, they could have walked on the ice or used dogs. But how did they get around in sloppy spring and fall? I can't imagine being confined to this tiny place with a bunch of children and no privacy. To this, add black flies and no running water, fire or sewage, and you'd have your hands full. When I get back to Yellowknife, I'll check out the details. Wow! What a find!"

Nadlak, which means "caribou crossing" in the Inuktitut language, was discovered accidently in 1985 by Douglas Stern, a resident of Cambridge Bay, Northwest Territories. Like us, Doug was canoeing the Burnside and stopped for lunch on the island. He knew he was on to something important when he saw the antlers and stone rings. Stern photographed the site and sent the pictures to the Prince of Wales Northern Heritage Centre in Yellowknife, which forwarded them to Bryan Gordon, an archaeologist for the National Museums of Canada.

During the summers of 1985 and 1986, Gordon and a team of archaeologists visited Nadlak and began an archaeological dig. Gordon believes the site is very unusual because it is only one of two inland locations in the Canadian arctic where winter homes have been discovered.

The Copper Inuit, prehistoric natives of this area, traditionally lived on the coast, where they hunted seals, whales and walrus. To live inland, they would have had to give up eating sea mammals and turned to eating caribou. Evidence unearthed at Nadlak suggests that is exactly what they did. But why?

One theory suggests that a period of very cold weather forced the Inuit south. What geologists refer to as the "little ice age" began around A.D.1400 and lasted 400 years. For fifty years following the start of the cold weather, evidence showed the island at Nadlak was a popular summer tent site for families hunting caribou. By A.D.1450, permanent housing began to appear. The area was abandoned around 1700.

During the summers of 1985 and 1986, Bryan Gordon's archaeologists excavated and rebuilt two of the structures with antlers. They discovered that one house had contained 4,400 antlers, which, they guessed, were originally arranged to make an open dome roof. The walls of the house were made by simply stacking the antlers together.

Gordon believes the Inuit lived in the antler houses in summer and in the stone houses in winter. "We've never unearthed winter dwellings this far inland before, certainly not a camp of this size," says Gordon in the autumn 1986 edition of *Inuktitut* magazine. "You find places where the people had camp fires or tent rings, but that's about all."[1]

Inuit elders from Bathurst Inlet knew about Nadlak but could provide no information about the names or customs of the people who once lived there. Artifacts unearthed at the site included fire starters, needle cases, soapstone pots, pottery, harpoons, wooden animal heads, and copper knives and ulus, which confirmed that the inhabitants were members of an ancient Copper Inuit band. Archaeologists also unearthed parts of a leather harness, which indicates the residents probably had dogs. Remains of a birch-bark basket revealed that the people traded goods with southern Indians who lived within the tree line.

As the scientists probed the remains, they discovered that each house had four complete stone floors built one on top of the other. They also discovered bones from an estimated one-hundred thou-

1. From *Inuktitut* magazine, No. 64, Autumn 1986. *Inuktitut* is published by The Department of Indian Affairs and Northern Development, Ottawa, Canada K1A 0H4. *Inuktitut* is presently published by the Inuit Tapirisat of Canada, Ottawa, Canada. Reproduced with the permission of the Minister of Supply and Services Canada, 1993.

sand caribou! These finds prove that Nadlak had been continually occupied for hundred of years, and that the people who lived there depended solely on caribou to survive. There seems to be no doubt that the caribou were the reason the Inuit stayed at Nadlak.

Says Gordon in the *Inuktitut* article, "Caribou could have provided people with everything needed to survive in a harsh land. Not only could they provide food, their fat was probably valuable to residents for lighting lamps and for cooking. The skins were likely used for tents, clothing and footwear. Bones could make needles and weapons while sinew could serve as sewing thread."

Though caribou are wonderful cold-water swimmers (their hollow fur keeps them from freezing), they prefer shallow water crossings like those around Nadlak. Enough arrowheads and lance tips were found at Nadlak to support the theory that they were speared from kayaks as they crossed the river.

Three hundred years after the Eskimos left Nadlak, the caribou continue to come here. When we arrived at the island on August 1, 1988, caribou fur left by thousands of migrating animals choked the shorelines far as the eye could see. In the summer of 1985, researchers at Nadlak saw an estimated forty thousand caribou cross the river. The arctic is as it was. The rituals of a thousand years are repeated again and again. Only our presence reveals the sameness and wonder of it all.

Delinquents in Canoes

IT WAS NEARLY MIDNIGHT when I heard the clanging of their canoe. Two clean-shaven men—correction, boys—unhappily stepped out of the beached Grumman and, with mild profanity, ambled up the trail into the bright light of our cheery campfire. "Hey, man, you got a map?" demanded a powerfully built tow-headed boy of about sixteen. "Cool it, Chad," said his friend. "What he means, sir, is that we lost our map and can't find the portage out of here."

"I see," I said, and placed another log on the glowing blaze, while the eight teen-agers in my crew quizzically looked on. "Why don't you guys have some cocoa and popcorn and tell us all about it," I suggested.

"Uh, thanks," said the smaller of the two—a dark-haired lad who said his name was Jeremy.

According to their story, the boys were part of a church group that was camped on Mora Lake in Minnesota's Boundary Waters Canoe Area, which was just east of our camp on Little Saganaga Lake. They had gone canoeing after supper, and "just for fun," had portaged into Little Sag. When darkness fell, they became confused and paddled around till they saw our fire.

I knew that no responsible leader would permit kids to go out at night without a map, compass and flashlight, let alone portage into another lake, so I pressed for details. Jeremy was quicker-tongued than Chad, and had ready answers. He said they had lost their map on the portage. And their flashlight had gotten wet and didn't work.

"You guys have life jackets?" I queried, knowing full well this was essential equipment. Chad looked expectantly at Jeremy who, with some uneasiness replied, "Uh, they're in the canoe. Yeah, we left 'em in the canoe."

I peered over the embankment and shined my flashlight into the belly of the Grumman. "I don't see any," I said, with doubtful concern.

"Yeah, well, we stuffed 'em under the seats so they wouldn't get dirty," said Jeremy smartly.

"Whatever," I nodded, suspecting there was much more to the story than was being told.

The boys accepted our offer of hot chocolate and popcorn, then pressed me again for a map. I showed them our location and said I had no maps to spare. Besides that, Little Saganaga Lake is a complicated mass of islands, bays and arms. Experienced navigators have trouble finding their way around it in daylight. Only an expert would try it at night! It was obvious these boys had no backwoods skills, so I suggested they stay with us until morning, then search out their group.

But the pair was adamant that they must get going. I looked at my watch; it was nearly 1 A.M. We'd come the full length of the Frost River that day, and would layover in camp tomorrow. We planned to sleep till ten, then prepare a leisurely pancake breakfast, after which we'd swim, fish and just lounge around. We were still high with the excitement of the challenging day and no one was very tired. It was a beautiful moonlit night, and my crew had never canoed after dark, so I asked if anyone wanted to paddle to the portage. A few said yes, so I agreed to guide the boys to Mora Lake.

Twenty minutes later, we came to the long portage that led to Mora Lake. I showed the boys where they were on the map, then gave them a candle and some matches so they could light their way along the trail. We shook hands and I wished them good luck.

Two days later, we left our campsite on Little Saganaga Lake and paddled north through Gabimichigami, Agamok and Mueller Lakes, into sprawling Ogishkemuncie Lake. It was on the Ogish portage that we encountered the "church group" to which Jeremy and Chad had said they belonged. A boy of about sixteen had just dropped his Grumman canoe squarely on a jutting rock and was being reprimanded by the leader. The kid swore at him and was punished with an hour's worth of chopping wood. I looked at the barely dented Grumman; it bore the logo of a well-known Minnesota camp for juvenile delinquents. I thought about the ill-mannered boys who had bothered us two nights before. Could it be? Hmmm . . . I approached the leader and introduced myself.

When the group leader began to explain, everything became clear. The boys had been a problem from the start of the trip. They hated the woods and fought the "required experience" with every breath. By the third day, their whining and uncooperative behavior had earned them so many hours of camp chores that they had no free time at all. The camp was structured so that violators must both complete their jail time and pay all accrued "chore penalties" before they are released back into society. The boys had figured the best way out of the work—and the wilderness—was to paddle out. So they had waited till everyone was asleep, then stole a canoe and paddled off into the night.

They had lied about everything, even their names. They actually had been camped on Elton Lake, about a mile from our campsite on Little Saganaga. The boys had known their crew was looping back to the Gunflint Trail via Gabimichigami and Ogishkemuncie Lakes, so they decided to head off in the opposite direction—toward Mora Lake—with hopes of hitting a road or trail they could follow back to civilization. All they knew was they wanted out of the woods. Beyond this, they probably had no plan.

The leader did not seem particularly concerned about the breakout. He was sure the pair would be apprehended in a day or two.

However, he was mildly ticked that the little criminals had stolen his wallet, which had $34 in it. Then he grinned broadly and added, "The idiots have no map or compass. They didn't even take any food! Probably figured they could buy it along the way," he chuckled. The man was certain the wilderness would teach them a lesson they would never forget.

It did!

About a year later, I saw the camp leader at a canoe event in Minneapolis and asked him for the rest of the story. Seems the boys became lost on Mora Lake and paddled around for hours in search of the portage. When they couldn't find it, they gave up in disgust and struck out overland, first taking care to pull their canoe into the woods where it wouldn't be seen. For two days, they wandered aimlessly in the forest, hoping to come upon a road or house. But all they saw was tree after tree and hordes of hungry mosquitoes. They had no food or water, or any idea where they were. After two days of wandering around in the bush, they were ready to surrender—that is, if they could find someone to surrender to!

Around noon on the third day, they emerged on the shore of Gillis Lake, where they waved down some passing canoeists and poured out their story. The kids pleaded with the canoeists to take them out, and promised they would cause no trouble. But the people were afraid of them (they must have looked awful!), and refused to come ashore. Instead, they told the boys to stay put—they would send help the next day when they reached the trail-head. Then, they tossed ashore some peanut butter and crackers, hard candy and powdered pistachio pudding, and paddled away.

The leader told me the kids cheered when the authorities arrived, and gave them no trouble at all. They were model citizens when they returned to camp, and they stayed that way for the duration of their term. "Did you recover your wallet?" I asked. "Yes," he beamed. "And the thirty-four dollars too. I think the kids discovered the real value of money on this trip!"

A decade later, I saw the leader again and asked him if he'd heard anything about "Chad" and "Jeremy."

"Matter-of-fact, no," he drawled with a smile. "But in my business that's good news!"

White Bear

Fʀᴏᴍ ᴍʏ Nᴏʀᴛʜ Kɴɪꜰᴇ River Journal, dated July 19, 1992:

This river is not at all what I expected. Rapids around every bend, and they are all huge ones that require inspection. We get out of the canoes at every drop and study the river. Sometimes we run, sometimes we line; but first, we look and talk. There are no defined portages, only occasional animal trails that peter out after a few dozen yards. Had I known this trip would be so difficult I never would have offered it through the Science Museum (of Minnesota). Thank God everyone likes this stuff and understands white water. No sign of people anywhere—not even a tent site or fire pit. Does anyone ever paddle the North Knife?

The ice went out real late this year so we'll probably see polar bears near Hudson's Bay. Doug Webber, owner of North Knife Lodge—and just about everything else around the town of Churchill—suggested we bring a gun. We did. Three of 'em! Tom Anderson has a beater 12-gauge Ithaca. Along with a box of lead slugs, he brought ten "plastic stinger" shells (proven effective on bears in the Churchill area) and five "fire-cracker" shells, which he says will either scare bears away or set the woods on fire. Ha! Dick Magnuson bought a new 760 Remington slug gun just for the trip, and I'm carrying my old Centennial .444 Marlin, with peep sights. I loaded up a batch of 275-grain Barnes bullets. Pretty minimal for bears I know, but I'm a good shot and I've killed a lot of tin cans with this gun.

God, I hope I don't have to shoot a bear!!

We're fifty miles into the trip and no sign of white bears anywhere. Actually, we don't figure on seeing any till we reach the Bay. Even then, it's doubtful we'll luck out and see one up close. For this reason, no one but me has bothered to load their gun. I've

been taking a lot of razzing about carrying a loaded rifle at this point in the trip, but I think it's stupid to haul around useless metal. If a dangerous condition develops I want to be able to act quickly. After all, I am the leader!

July 20:

Coming around a bend, my partner Joanie points and says, "Hey, Cliff, look at that mountain goat up there." Seconds later the goat transmutes into a full-grown male polar bear, who slides down the bank and swims straight toward our canoe.

"Backferry!" I yell. "Jesus Christ, backferry!" It's like we're paddling through glue, and the bear keeps coming! Luckily, when he's barely fifty feet away, the powerful current sweeps him around the bend. Will he come ashore and crash back through the bush at us? Soon as the boat touches land, I'm out, rifle in hand and praying I won't have to shoot. Seconds later, Dick and Finette arrive, sheet white. Suddenly, it turns into a comedy—everyone massed in a tiny group, scared as hell, me clutching the half-cocked Marlin while Dick drops shotgun slugs into the sand and Tom gropes in his pack for the plastic stinger shells. We're seventy-five miles from the bay and no one but me is ready to shoot. What a rush!

Saw three more bears later—two swimming, one on land. Bear tracks everywhere. We arranged tents like a fort. Perimeter teams have capsican (bear mace). I served everyone double shots of Pusser's rum tonight.

Later:

Twenty miles from Hudson's Bay we came upon Doug Webber's hunting cabin. The windows were heavily barred and huge spikes protruded from the door—testimony to the destructive power of polar bears. We saw another cabin at Hudson's Bay—a decrepit goose-hunting shack that had been invaded by curious bears. Everything—cots, carpeting, you name it—had been torn to shreds. We climbed on to the roof to get a better view of the ocean and promptly saw two more bears. After that, no one went out hiking without a gun.

At three A.M. the next morning, we paddled into a red rising sun and the misty saltwater of Hudson's Bay. Rounding the point, we saw scores of porpoising beluga whales. And three more bears!

Good Mechanic, Good Shower

M OST MECHANICS RELY on systematic trial-and-error to solve problems. They figure if they replace enough parts, they'll eventually find the difficulty. At the other extreme are a small number of experts who, like my friend Chic Sheridan, have the uncanny ability to quickly and correctly diagnose problems on complex machines they've never seen before. For example, I once purchased an old Ford Pinto at an auction for next to nothing. The car had a horrible clanging sound, which was diagnosed by one mechanic as stuck valves. Repairs would cost hundreds of dollars!

I drove the beast over to Chic's house, hopeful he could provide a less-costly diagnosis. "Add a quart of tranny fluid to the crankcase every time you change oil," he suggested. "Old mechanics trick—should free those valves in minutes. Works much better than anything you can buy."

Chic's advice was sound. I drove the old Ford for two years, then traded it for another beater.

On another occasion, a friend asked me to ask Chic about a clutch problem in her 1980 Saab. A mechanic in a local foreign car repair shop told us the throw-out bearing and clutch plate were bad. "Cost you about six-hundred bucks," grinned the mechanic.

Chic had never owned or driven a foreign car. A strong union man all his life, he supported the "buy American" philosophy, and believed cars from overseas were trash. So it came as quite a surprise when he agreed to look at the old Saab.

The engine compartment of the Saab was a nightmare of wires, boxes and hoses. I was certain it would take a trained Saab mechanic just to find the clutch, let alone fix it. Chic peered under the hood.

"I see someone just put a new master cylinder in here," he drawled. "Yeah, two weeks ago," I affirmed. There was a long silence. Then, "Well I'll be damned, the idiot never hooked up the hydraulic line!" Chic shook his head in disgust, grabbed some tools, and a few minutes later the car shifted fine. Cost of repair? Two beers and a "Thanks, good buddy!".

Chic was also an inventor and master welder. He made me the stainless steel grill I use on all my canoe trips, and a quarter-inch thick aluminum griddle that fits on my trail stove. He also designed the best canoe trailer I've ever owned. For Christmas one year, he gave all his canoeing friends collapsible wood-framed bucksaws that he had built in his own shop.

Chic earned his living as a maintenance chief in an ammonia plant just south of St. Paul, Minnesota. He hated the work, often saying he wished he could have gone to college and become a forester or wildlife professional. Chic's heart and soul were in the forests of northern Minnesota and Ontario. He fished, camped and canoed with his friends every chance he got.

Socially, Chic lived in two worlds—the blue-collar environment of his work place and the white-collar social circle of his college-educated canoeing friends. Chic valued education and was envious of our advanced degrees, though we never mentioned them. On every trip he would remind us that he had been a poor student in high school, then question why we included him in our lofty group. At this, like little kids, we'd reinforce the obvious: "Because we love you and respect you and think you're wonderful." Then we'd pass around some peppermint schnapps and toast the most important person on any backwoods trip —the one who could keep the truck running, fix the trail stove, mend broken equipment and keep us entertained with bad jokes for hours. "To Chic," I would call. Everyone would shout, "Here, here," and the bottle would go around again.

Chic didn't cuss very much. Except for the occasional "dammit" or "sonufabitch," he was clean-lipped. This was in stark contrast to two members of our fraternity who swore constantly. Chic never said anything about the foul language—that is, until he gave us the shower bag.

We were about to canoe the Fond du Lac River in northern Saskatchewan when a family emergency forced Chic to drop out. There was time to find a replacement, but it wouldn't be the same. Besides, we knew how Chic looked forward to these annual trips. So we took up a collection and bought him a new life jacket—a brilliant gold model that was state-of-the-art for paddling white water.

Chic was touched by the gift, and a week later, he presented us with one of his own. "It's a solar camping shower," he grinned. "Now you guys can finally clean up your act!"

The apparatus consisted of a black plastic bag, a long delivery tube and shower head. You could fill the bag directly with hot water or set it in the sun for a few hours. The shower seemed like a good idea, so we agreed to take it along.

The unit worked as advertised—that is, when we could find a solid support for it. Five liters of water weighs more than ten pounds—an uneasy, slippery load to be raised above our heads each night. First, we'd look for a high rock ledge that was wide enough to hold the bag. Failing that, we'd search for a strong tree limb. Tall pines and birches were abundant on the eskers, but were otherwise nonexistent.

What to do? In desperation, we lashed together a tripod of canoe paddles, then carefully balanced the bloated water bag on top. Since the bag was barely three feet off the ground, we had to stoop low, or lie down to get enough water pressure to produce a steady flow. The procedure worked okay when the bag was full, but not when the the supply was half-exhausted. Once the bag lost its shape, it came splashing down.

After several frustrating trials, we decided the only way to ensure adequate water pressure—and our own safety—was to have one person hold the water bag on top of the tripod while another took a shower. This method proved reliable, so we adopted it as policy. But after a week of watching each other bathe, we gave up on the shower, agreeing never to let Chic know how much we hated it.

A few weeks after the trip, we gathered at Chic's house for a party and slide show. As we flipped through the pictures, we paused extra long on those that showed the shower. Finally, we came to our tripod, and proudly asked Chic what he thought of it.

Chic knocked the ashes out of his corncob pipe and took a long deep draw on his beer. Then, with a deadpan expression he asked, "Why didn't you guys just put the bag on the ground and step on it? Then, you wouldn't have had to build that silly thing every night!"

Chic Sheridan died of ALS (Lou Gehrig's disease) on February 20, 1987. He was 67 years old.

White Otter Castle

CHIC SHERIDAN AND I found White Otter Castle by accident in 1984 while canoeing the Turtle River near Ignace, Ontario.

We'd been pinned for hours in a rocky cove off White Otter Lake by a fierce east wind that kicked up man-sized rollers. We knew our tiny solo canoes were no match for the pounding water, so we agreed to strike out again after dark, when the wind was down. Just after midnight, we paddled out into knee-high waves and set course for a protected spot on the leeward shore of a peninsula where we would be sheltered from the morning wind.

Twenty minutes later we were across the mile-wide expanse of open water and cruising down the moonlit shoreline. In the distance, we saw what appeared to be a huge log tower. Regardless, it was worth investigating, if for no other reason than there was probably a flat place to camp nearby.

As we neared the tower, it grew into a full-blown log mansion. The main building had three levels and was twice as long as my fifteen-foot canoe. The tower was four stories high and had windows all around. A long porch fronted both the main building and the attached cabin-sized room that we later learned was the kitchen. The entire dwelling was artfully assembled from giant red pine logs that must have weighed nearly a ton a piece. "I'd like to meet the knight who lived in this castle," said Chic dryly.

We unfurled our sleeping bags beneath the overhang of the sagging porch and settled in for the night. In the morning, we decided, we'd have a closer look at this castle in the wilderness.

After breakfast, we spent several hours probing the structure, which might best be described as a cross between a sprawling ranch house and a horse barn. The logs were so huge we assumed that horses, winches and skids must have been used to move and raise them. Meticulous detail work suggested there had been a skilled carpenter on hand. Corner logs had been masterfully dove-tailed into place—a far cry from the axe-notched fit of the typical bush cabin. Each log had been hewn square on three sides for a perfect fit before it was chinked with a mixture of lime and sand. There were twenty-six carefully fitted windows, all secured in store-bought sashes. How on earth had they gotten here? No roads led to the castle, so everything must have been brought in by canoe from Ignace and packed over a dozen or more portages—an impossible feat for a single man. For a long time, Chic and I just stood on the beach and marveled at this mansion in the back-woods. When we finished our canoe trip, we decided we'd stop in Ignace and check out the history of the place. There was enough graffiti on the walls to suggest the castle was not a well-kept secret.

Our research was fruitful—it turned out the castle had an inter-esting past, as did its owner and builder, Jimmy McQuat.

A Scotch immigrant, McQuat built the castle for a Scotch noblewoman he loved. Evidently, she agreed to marry him if he would build for her a "proper house" in the wilderness.

But Jimmy McQuat apparently never married his lady love, for at the age of 31, he advertised for a mail-order bride to share his wilderness life. His ad, reprinted in *White Otter Castle: the legacy of Jimmy McQuat* by Elinor Barr, is dated July 22, 1887, and states that he doesn't drink, smoke or swear. "I have not much learning but I have morality and character to make up. I would like a girl under 27 years, not too thundering big, brought up on a farm . . . Her hair may be any colour but firery red."[1]

Within the year, Jane Gibson of Clifford, Ontario, agreed to marry Jimmy, provided he'd come to Clifford and meet her family. But Jimmy refused to go and the wedding never took place. Jane was Jimmy's last attempt to find a wife.

Though Jimmy McQuat lived a solitary life, we discovered he was not a hermit. He was a good conversationalist and he enjoyed entertaining friends. For awhile, he even served on the local school board. Unlike most of his friends, Jimmy was able to make a good

1. *White Otter Castle: the legacy of Jimmy McQuat,* is a Northwestern Ontario heritage publication. It is available for $5.00 from Singing Shield Productions, 104 Ray Blvd., Thunder Bay, Ontario, Canada P7B 4C4.

living. He came from a long line of proud Scottish farmers who knew how to work the land and invest money. A prudent business-man, Jimmy once owned two farms and a half-section of prime Ontario land. Then, when the gold rush peaked in 1899, he got gold fever and sold everything to follow his dream. A year later he had lost everything and had to start over again.

In 1903, Jimmy staked out a new homestead on the north shore of White Otter Lake, the present site of the castle. He built a small cabin, grew a vegetable garden and trapped, and took odd jobs to make ends meet. But as the years wore on, Jimmy was plagued by the childhood memory of an angry blacksmith who told him he'd "die in a shack." By God, he'd show the blacksmith. He'd build a castle in the wilderness!

Jimmy McQuat began work on his dream home in 1914, at the age of fifty-nine. The huge red pine logs, which averaged thirty-seven feet when cut, were felled within three-hundred yards of the site, and were dragged to position using a homemade winch. Jimmy cut, trimmed and fit every log into place without the help of machines, horses or friends. I remember marveling at the pre-cise fit of the huge pine beams. Even with a winch and other equipment, it seems impossible he could have raised the logs and fitted the dovetails alone.

Jimmy McQuat died as he had lived, quietly and alone. Evidently, he drowned while netting fish off his dock during the ice melt of early spring. Several months later, forest rangers found his body and buried it beside the tower.

As the years have passed, weather and time have taken their toll on the abandoned castle. The porch sags, chinking has fallen from between the logs and the rain seeps in through the roof. But it's still a remarkable monument to the frontier spirit. In 1983, the cas-tle was made part of the Turtle River Waterway Park, sparking the hope that Jimmy McQuat's dream may one day be restored to its original grandeur.

Inquiries about the castle should be directed to: District Manager—Ministry of Natural Resources, 108 Saturn Ave., Atikokan, Ontario, Canada P0T 1C0.

The Voyage of the Blue Canoe

O N THE FOURTH DAY of our canoe trip down Ontario's Kopka River, we came upon "the rapid." Snuggled in the thick spruce of a long s-curve, the rushing water at the top looked manageable. A portage began in a quiet bay well above the drop but the trail was so poorly marked and overgrown that we thought the pitch might be runnable. But it never pays to assume anything on a canoe trip, so we put ashore and struggled through tangled alders to a small rock outcrop where we could see around the bend. "My God, will you look at that," gulped my partner, pointing to the foaming white water and mass of jumbled boulders that clogged the river.

"No way," I said. "Let's portage!"

We decided to take a shortcut back to the boats, and thereby get the inevitable bushwhacking out of the way as quickly as possible. I figured the quickest route back was to beeline for the portage (which appeared to parallel the rapid), then follow the portage back to its start. So I set my compass accordingly, and struck out through the bush, confident we'd intercept the trail in a matter of yards. Five minutes passed, then ten, and no sign of a trail. I realized the portage had angled north over the ridge, so I gave the order to abandon ship and retrace our steps. Minutes later, we were back at the trailhead, psyched for the half-mile carry.

It was a sweltering 90° and raining mosquitoes when the last of our gear was brought to the end of the portage, which to our surprise was in a mucky cove a quarter-mile below the foot of the rapid. As the ten of us milled around the tight little landing, sweating and swatting bugs while we waited for our turn to cast off, some crew members passed the time by playing a provocative game of "What if?"

What if we could have lined or portaged around the bad water at the top of the rapid, then safely ran the rest? What if there was an easier portage on river right? What if we had run the pitch and capsized in the maelstrom—a cool bath would feel great in this heat! What if, somehow, we could've done this drop!

If you've done much wilderness canoeing, you are probably familiar with these bold scenarios, which always develop after everyone and everything is out of danger.

"Okay, you guys," I said. "Let's go have a look at this measly rapid then."

Seven minutes of flat-water paddling brought us to the base of the drop, which emptied into a quiet pool in a hidden bay of Kenakskaniss Lake. The river ended here in a series of small falls and waist-high boulders—an impossible run.

For awhile, we played in the powerful currents below the boulder line, ferrying from eddy to eddy, surfing the wave trains, splashing each other with our paddles and generally having a great time, all the while congratulating ourselves on our wise decision to portage. Then, someone noticed a splash of blue on the far shore that looked like a canoe. Curious, we paddled over for a closer look.

Indeed it was a canoe—or rather the front half of a once-proud eighteen-foot Jensen cruiser—a fast, easy-paddling lake canoe that has no whitewater capabilities. The torn fiberglass hull was propped on a huge boulder, perhaps as a sign warning others they must portage or perish!

Jeff Janacek and I went ashore for a closer look. The front bucket seat, hardware and side walls were still intact. So was the 1978 Minnesota boat registration sticker. Jeff, an aspiring landscape photographer, earns his living as a criminal investigator in a metropolitan police department. He's earned a reputation among his colleagues as a "Dick Tracy"; he can solve any mystery.

"Whatcha think, Jeff? Sticker's twelve years old—can you find out the story on this canoe?" I asked hopefully.

Jeff smiled confidently, pulled out a small notebook, and began to write. "It will receive my personal, professional attention," he asserted.

Several weeks later, Jeff shared his findings in a letter:

"The investigation began with the old canoe's registration number," he wrote. "I requested a detailed search of public microfilm records to determine who had registered the Wenonah canoe in

1978. Not only was I fortunate enough to identify the bow paddler and former owner of the craft, but I learned he still lived in the same place noted on his old registration and had the same phone number. It would appear that in at least some respects, canoeists are more stable than most of the people I investigate. The owner enthusiastically recounted the near-fatal event that resulted in the broken blue canoe, but requested anonymity. His story has important lessons for everyone who paddles the bush rivers of Canada."

The man told Janacek that he and three friends had been planning to canoe the Kopka River for some time. Everyone in the party was an accomplished lake paddler, with preferences for lean, fast canoes. The men had been repeatedly warned by experts that the quick Jensens they used on the lakes of the Boundary Waters were out of place on a wild Canadian river, where rapids and quick turns were the rule. But the men disregarded the advice, arguing that the Jensens would do fine as long as they were portaged around rapids.

As the days on the river wore on, the two crews became increasingly competitive. When one team of paddlers took the lead, they stretched it to the limit, often disappearing in a hail of spray around the next bend. Getting there first became as important as getting there at all.

On that fateful day in 1978, the men in the blue canoe were far ahead of their friends. They powered around the bend that marked the start of the rapid (it was on the map), missing the obscure portage, and entered the slick water above the first drop. As soon as the canoeists realized they had gone too far, they eddied out of the main current and turned around, intent on paddling back upstream to calm water. But the deep, fine ends of the Jensen caught the eddy line, and the craft capsized, spilling both men into the frigid water.

The bow man hung onto a pack as long as his cold-numbed hands would allow, then he succumbed to the power of the rapid. His life jacket, which was not completely zipped, buoyed up and prevented the back of his head from being bruised by rocks. He was sure he was going to die, even after the rapid washed him out at the bottom. There he floated, too cold and tired to swim to shore.

Meanwhile, the man's partner held on to the canoe until it broke up in the rocks—"Until there wasn't anything big enough to hang on to"—then, he pulled himself out of the water in an eddy halfway down the falls and attempted to find his way through the woods to the portage that angled over the ridge a quarter-mile away!

Unaware their friends were in trouble, the men in the second canoe started the portage. They completed the half-mile carry without seeing either of their companions. Then they paddled out into the lake in search of the blue canoe which, they believed, was still in the lead.

After an hour of searching for their friends, the second team returned to the portage, thinking the others had made a wrong turn. Here, they found the stern paddler of the blue canoe. Between hypothermic shivers, the frozen canoeist told his friends he'd lost track of his partner when the canoe broke apart.

Hearing this, the canoeists provided dry clothes for the hypothermic fellow, and beat a hasty course for the foot of the rapid where, to their horror, they discovered the other man floating glassy-eyed in an eddy. He could neither move nor talk—an hour's exposure to the icy water had no doubt lowered his body temperature to a dangerous, almost irreversible point. To make matters worse, what had been a chilling rain turned to sleet as the air temperature plummeted to near freezing—in all, perfect conditions for death by hypothermia!

Only the quick thinking of the two healthy canoeists saved the lives of the others. They moved the two victims to a protected rock outcrop at the foot of the rapid, where they built a huge fire and concentrated on treating the hypothermia. Then, they discussed how they might complete the remaining twenty-two miles of the trip in one canoe. They had seen no one since they started out two weeks earlier. It was unreasonable to think help was just around the bend.

When the hypothermia victims were able to travel, the crew built log outriggers for the remaining canoe, with hopes the craft could then accommodate four passengers and gear. Everyone piled into the craft and they nosed the canoe into the waves of Kenakskaniss Lake. But the little boat began to take on water, so the men returned to shore to formulate a new plan. They decided to ferry three men across the eight-mile lake, drop off one at the portage, then return for the fourth. With three paddles churning, the shuttle should have taken less than four hours.

About an hour after the canoe was out of sight, the remaining man spotted a fishing boat and waved it down. The kind-hearted fishermen warmed him, then took him to the portage, where he rejoined his friends. The four completed the trip in the single canoe, leaving the blue canoe where it lay at the base of the falls.

Twelve years after the life-threatening incident, the bow man of the demolished Jensen remembered every detail of the "voyage of the blue canoe." He told Jeff Janacek in no uncertain terms that he was lucky to be alive, that he intended to stay that way, and that he would never, ever, canoe another whitewater river in Canada!

At the foot of a lonely rapid near Kenakskaniss Lake on the Kopka River, the remains of a blue canoe stand sentry to his promise.

Foresters Don't Get Lost!

A T THE OUTSET, I should make it perfectly clear that what I did was stupid. Incredibly stupid! But I was barely twenty-one at the time and my brain wasn't fully formed. I was fresh out of college and working as a forester for the Bureau of Land Management in Coos Bay, Oregon, when it happened. A team of foresters had just finished marking a timber sale when they discovered the cutting boundary line crossed some private land. The land owner demanded that the line be changed immediately, and I was given the task of doing it.

The cutting boundary ran through deep wilderness and was marked every fifty feet or so with yellow plastic flagging. I'd have to tear off the old ribbons and establish a new perimeter—a task that would take a couple days. I parked the Jeep in a narrow cut off the main road and assembled my gear. In the pockets of my vest I carried a compass and a roll of plastic flagging, my lunch and Thermos, a pocket knife and matches. The project seemed simple enough, so I left my map on the seat of the jeep. After all, any numb brain could follow a ribbon line!

The master map in the office showed that the cutting line began at the gravel road where I was parked. It followed a ridge west for about a mile, then curved north and ended at a dirt spur that led to a paved road a dozen miles away. Unless I planned to hike twelve miles to the blacktop, plus twenty more to the Jeep, I'd have to return by the route I came. Logically, I had to follow the ribbons to the spur and collect them on the hike back. That would be enough work for one day. Then, a brilliant thought emerged: Why not pull ribbons on the way in? What I missed, I could get when I came back. If portions of the route became confusing, I'd simply abandon my plan and let the yellow plastic guide me home. Besides, it was Friday and elk season opened the following day. So the sooner I finished the job, the faster I could get to my hunting area.

The folly of my plan never occurred to me as I started out. I confidently plodded up the hill, pulling yellow ribbons as I went. But when I reached the ridge and stopped, looking back, I fleetingly questioned the sanity of my procedure. But it was a hot, sunny day and I was anxious to go hunting, so I threw logic to the wind and kept pulling off ribbons.

The ridge provided easy walking, and I covered its one-mile length in less than an hour—a fast pace for cruising the woods around Coos Bay. My pockets bulged with yellow plastic ribbon—much more ribbon, I thought, than was necessary to mark such an easy trail. I remember thinking that anyone who needed yellow markers to follow a ridge didn't belong in the woods! Then I fantasized that I, a 21-year-old forester from Indianapolis, had more woods sense than the loggers who made their living here. Two hours later, I would have a somewhat different opinion of myself.

The ridge ended at a deep ravine, and the flagged trail turned north and descended into a shallow valley, where it bobbed and twisted around huge fir trees and dense brush. Luscious vegetation consumed every space, and transpiration mist rose skyward, driven by the blazing sun. I was back in "machete country" again, where visibility was measured in feet. I knew that if I got lost, I'd never be found!

Break time: I sat down, lit a cigarette (I have long since quit this disgusting habit) and poured a cup of coffee. I remembered the horror story about the man who, just a year earlier, had parked his car along a secondary road near Coos Bay, then walked into the woods to relieve himself and disappeared. His family shouted for him for hours but there was no reply. Four weeks later, authorities found his remains 100 yards from the road!

I also recalled the tale about the million-dollar meteorite that landed deep in the Douglas fir forest outside Coos Bay. An elderly geologist discovered it and immediately organized a team to bring it out. But the man died of a heart attack on the hike in, and the treasure was never found—despite the fact its location was supposedly pinpointed to within twenty square miles. Sixty years later, treasure hunters still search for the "lost meteorite."

I glanced at my watch: it was 9:30 A.M. "Better get moving, Cliff," I muttered aloud. I carefully field-stripped my cigarette, shoved my Thermos back into my cruiser's vest, and descended into the fog-filled valley below. I plucked a yellow ribbon from the branch of a huge rhododendron bush, paused momentarily and looked skyward. The towering Douglas fir trees shut out every ray of sun. Indeed, the crown cover was so dense that if I became lost, I would not be able to signal or see an airplane. Even a smoky fire would not cut through the thick mist. The question was, *could I find my way home without the flagging to guide me?*

Deep down, I suspected I couldn't, but I'd made a decision and I had my pride! By God, I'd show 'em what a "woodchuck" from Indianapolis could do! So I stubbornly continued northward, pulling the flags as I walked. The trail went up, then down—it wound around huge fallen trees and boulders. Except for the fact that it went roughly north and was mostly on the level, there was no sense to it at all.

Fifteen minutes passed since I'd left the ridge, then half an hour. By now, I realized I was doing a very stupid thing. Yet, I could not stop pulling off those ribbons. I was determined to complete what I had begun, no matter the consequences. The longer I hiked, the more stubborn I became.

It was a few minutes past noon when I came to the logging spur, where I ate lunch and pondered my situation. For the first time since I'd left the ridge I knew where I was. I could follow the spur to the highway, then hitch a ride back to the Jeep . . . Or, return through the woods the way I came. It would take about four hours to hike to the blacktop, and who knows how much longer to get a ride. If I followed my path back, and everything went according to plan, I could be back at the rig by six.

On the other hand, I had collected all the plastic flagging. Why retrace old ground when I could simply follow a southeast compass course back to the Jeep? As the crow flies, it couldn't be more than two miles. Besides, the idea of hiking through uncharted forest with a compass and no map, intrigued me. It had become a challenge I could not refuse. "Great idea!" I thought. "I'll hike cross-country and be out of the woods by two!"

Confidently, I set the compass and sallied forth. Ten minutes later, I was in trouble, for ahead gaped a ravine that a mountain goat could not traverse. For the first time since I'd started, I cussed myself for leaving my map behind. Well, the only solution was to parallel the cut until I could find a way around it. Two hours later,

I did, and again turned southeast. An hour later, I came to an impassable wall of brush and downed trees that I couldn't get around. At this point, I backtracked west, hopeful of intersecting the valley that I had followed to the spur road. But I missed it, and kept hiking deeper and deeper into the woods.

I glanced at my watch. It was 6:15 P.M. and I had no idea where I was! I panicked and began to run. Seconds later, I tripped over a vine and sprawled into a mass of thick ferns. I was lost. Really lost!

I lit a cigarette and allowed my muddled brain to clear. I had no idea where I was, and I was so far off course that I could not calculate a bearing to either the road or the logging spur. Logging roads, by definition, cannot have more than a ten-percent grade, which, in the Coast Range of Oregon, means they switchback to ascend hills. "Damn!" I cussed. "If only I had my map!"

Then, there was the cruel reality that it would be dark in two hours and I would probably have to spend the night in the bush. Government employees don't work on Saturday or Sunday, and I had Monday and Tuesday off for hunting. No one would even think of searching for me till Wednesday, when I didn't report for work. Even then, they would probably dismiss my absence, figuring I was still rerouting the old cutting line. Why, they might not even look for me until the office meeting on Friday! I realized I could easily spend a lonely week in the woods before a search was mounted. Even then, with the topography and canopy cover, I might never be found.

Ultimately, I concluded that my best shot was to head west, toward the ocean and U.S. Highway 101, which was about sixty miles away. I figured I could make about ten miles a day, which would bring me to the black top in a week. I had one sandwich, an apple and a candy bar. Water was everywhere: after all, this was a rain forest! I might be worse for wear when I got out, but I would survive. I would not die in the Coast Range!

At this, a great calm fell over me. Clearheaded now, I oriented myself using my compass, and headed toward the ocean.

Submerged in layers of brush, I slept (off and on) that first night under the towering branches of a huge Douglas fir, then continued to hike when the sun came up. On Saturday night, I found a small ledge that I lined with ferns and evergreen boughs. I was surprisingly calm and confident—I even took time to weave a sleeping bag of sorts from vegetation that I cut with my pocket knife. I was proud of my warm and comfortable bed and felt that I was "growing" with the experience. What the day before had been a nightmare was now a challenge.

At this point, food was my greatest concern. I knew I needed energy to maintain the pace, so from the start, I had rationed the remains of my lunch. Breakfast on Sunday was half an apple and one-third of a giant Butterfinger. After this, all that remained was a small piece of the candy bar. I knew the area was ringed with logging roads. Hopefully, I'd hit one today, before I got too hungry.

At eleven o'clock on Monday morning, I walked into the blazing sunlight of an old clear-cut. A maze of roads led out of the long-abandoned operation, and I picked one that headed roughly west. Five hours later, I came to a well-maintained two-lane gravel road, which I followed with great enthusiasm. Within the hour, a logging truck came by and I flagged it down. The driver took one look at me and asked if I wanted to go to a hospital. "No, I'm just tired and hungry," I replied. Then, I asked him if he'd take me back to my Jeep, which, I learned, was forty miles away.

The trucker didn't even question the request. He just gave me an orange, which I devoured instantly, then spun the fully loaded rig around and drove me where I wanted to go. I offered to pay him for the taxi service, but he adamantly refused. We parted with warm smiles and a hearty handshake.

I began to fall asleep as soon as I started driving. Indeed, I was so tired I couldn't keep my eyes on the road. The nearest place where I could get food and lodging was just forty miles away, but I wasn't sure I could make it. I stopped at least five times and doused myself with water from the big canteen in the Jeep; I slapped my face repeatedly and sang aloud.

At about 6 P.M., I wheeled into a seedy motel on the outskirts of a small logging town. I took a room, then wobbled over to the adjacent cafe for a much-needed meal. I had never been so hungry in my life. The smells of the cooking food exploded visions in my mind. Chicken, fried chicken—the wonderful odor of it overwhelmed me. I ordered a giant cola and two fried chicken dinners.

"Two?" asked the waitress, with a perplexed look. "Two," I mumbled authoritatively.

I consumed both dinners in a matter of minutes then waddled back to the motel where I attempted to shower and shave. But I was so dizzy I could not stand up in the shower, so I cleansed myself sitting down. I tried to shave, but felt like I was going to pass out every time I stood up. Then, I suddenly became dreadfully sick and threw up everything I had eaten. I washed my face and miserably crawled beneath the blankets, where I fell into a deep, numb sleep that lasted fourteen hours.

After a modest breakfast of steak and eggs, with a giant tomato juice and double order of hash browns, I quietly drove back to my home outside Coos Bay. It was mid-afternoon when I pulled into the driveway, and I was tired again. I hit the sack and slept till 9 A.M., then I ate again—some soup and hamburgers.

I reported to work as usual on Wednesday morning, and was dutifully asked if I had shot an elk. "Nyah, didn't even see one," I replied, with an air of disappointment. Then I told my boss I had removed the old flagging and would put in the new cutting line on Thursday.

Until ten years ago, I had never told anyone—not even my closest friends—about my ordeal in the Oregon woods.

Why?

Because foresters don't get lost!

Canoeing the Hood River to the Arctic Sea

THEY FEED SILENTLY, moving in a great undulating wave across the endless tundra. Momentarily, one looks up at us and snorts heavily. But there is no fear or real concern. They sense we are no threat. We stand confidently at the edge of this great herd of caribou, which stretches northward as far as the eye can see. The animals boldly come within a canoe length of our continuously clicking cameras. Kent Swanson excitedly snaps picture after picture. Only when he reloads his camera does he realize he has neglected to focus a single shot!

These caribou—we estimate there are ten to fifteen-thousand—are part of a much larger herd of ninety-seven thousand. The migration begins in early summer; each year the great herds move southward toward warmer wintering grounds, just as their ancestors have done for millennia.

Reb Bowman runs south across the ridge. "They're swimming across the lake," he yells, but in the confusion no one hears his words but me. Out of film, I work my way back to the lake and the beached canoe. Ahead are three large brown shapes. Musk ox? I sink to my knees and crawl through the tangled heather of the tundra. When I am within fifty yards of the mysterious forms, I raise myself for a closer look. *Grizzlies!* Three of them—a big sow and two half-grown yearlings. All I can think is, "Grizzlies are unpredictable!" Slowly, I retreat, but it's too late.

The she-bear sees me and stands up, big as a house! She sniffs the air curiously, then drops to all fours and gallops toward me, cubs in tow. I want to run but know better. I want to scream, but can't. Terrified, I roll into a ball in the spongy tundra, clasp my

hands behind my neck . . . and play dead. The bears come within a few feet, catch my scent, then scamper off leaving me unharmed. I thank God for intervening in my behalf.

Speechless and floating high on a cloud of intense emotion, I amble on rubber legs toward the safety of my canoe. Suddenly, all the hardship of "getting here" have been eclipsed by this single momentous experience. The trip has barely begun and already it exceeds my greatest expectations.

The Hood River begins just northeast of Takijak Lake at the edge of the Arctic Circle. From here, it flows swiftly north 180 miles through the most remote part of Canada's Northwest Territories, ultimately terminating at Bathurst Inlet on the Arctic Ocean.

Our intent was to spend a month canoeing the Arctic, which meant beginning our trip well south of the Hood River. We decided to start at Obstruction Rapids on Point Lake, some two-hundred miles below the river. From here, we'd proceed "uphill" through a chain of lakes and small streams, ultimately crossing the high point about a hundred miles (or a week) into the trip. We anticipat-

ed that the upstream portion of the route would be grueling, with portages totalling as much as three miles (unfortunately, we were right on target in this prediction). However, it would be worth the effort if for no other reason than to toughen our skills for the river. Also, our Canadian Land Use maps, which include detailed informaton about fish and wildlife, geology and ecology, indicated that this area was a primary migration route for caribou, and we didn't want to miss seeing these animals.

As our research for the trip continued, an unsettling fact emerged. To reach the Hood, we'd have to paddle the entire fifty-mile length of Takijak Lake. If our luck held, we would find ourselves battling a fierce north wind. If it didn't, there would be ice—lots of it. The north end of Takijak sometimes remains ice-bound all summer long. In mid-July of 1979, a Canadian team was stopped cold here by pack-ice. Our anticipated arrival date was July 31, 1982. But they were fortunate—an unexpected gale blew the lake clear within a day. We could only hope for similar good fortune.

Our schedule was tight. If we were to reach the Arctic Ocean by August 19, as planned, we could afford to wait no more than a few days for ice to clear from Takijak. If worse came to worse, we could paddle west across the lake and into the Fairy River. From there, we could thread our way into the Coppermine River, and finish at the Eskimo settlement of Coppermine. It would be a big disappointment, but would be "a way out."

We arrived at Yellowknife, where we would catch our flight in, on July 18, only to discover that all planes were grounded due to bad weather. We spent the day exploring the spectacular Museum of the North and shopping for Eskimo art.

Yellowknife is a town you can fall in love with: It's ultra modern, with paved streets, underground malls and a few mini-skyscrapers. There are fancy restaurants, a movie theater and a huge indoor swimming pool. And the people—a mixture of whites, Indians and Inuit (Eskimos)—are among the friendliest anywhere.

The following morning, the skies cleared sufficiently for us to fly. However, the fierce north wind continued, making it impossible to land at our proposed "put-in" below Obstruction Rapids. Instead, the pilot chose to land in a quiet cove about fifteen miles from the rapids on Point Lake.

Immediately we were wind-bound—a condition repeated daily, off and on, for the next two weeks. By 10 P.M., the waves subsided enough to allow us to wet our paddles in the 39° waters of the lake. The first week, we traveled mostly at night when the wind was down (there are about 22 hours of daylight at this latitude), sleeping when we could. The nearly continuous wind brought with it one respite—no bugs!

Our schedule required us to average about 13 miles a day—a feat that should have required little effort. But the high winds and frequent portages of up to two-and-a-half miles (three carries at the start!) pushed us behind schedule. To regain lost time, we paddled at every opportunity, often sleeping only four hours a night. Our persistence paid off. By July 27, we were back on schedule . . . and wind-bound in a quiet, bug-infested cove on Rockinghorse Lake.

The route out of Rockinghorse was a killer. This was smallstream work—wading through icy water and frequent, strenuous portaging. Whenever the river narrowed to a single line on our 1:250,000 maps, there was a carry. And there were a lot of single lines along the route. We put getting to the river out of mind. We wondered if we'd even reach Takijak.

The wind grew stronger as we moved north. We were now grateful for the shelter of the small streams. Nevertheless, we were soon wind-bound again, this time at the edge of an insignificant pond.

We fixed a hasty lunch of soup and pilot biscuits in the shelter of an overturned canoe and for awhile just sat around, not fully believing our progress could be stopped on a lake no larger than a football field. Reb Bowman checked the wind gauge—forty miles per hour! The sky was deep gray—no break in sight. Beaten by the weather, we pitched our tents on a small level spot at the top of a nearby esker and battened down for the worst.

With each passing hour the wind grew fiercer. The tents shivered violently, snapping and cracking so loudly that it was impossible to sleep. Wind speed had increased to fifty miles an hour. We prayed the tents would hold!

Forty-eight hours later, the storm subsided and we ventured from our nylon shelters to survey the damage. Tents, canoes, gear—everything was intact and unharmed. We could paddle again!

As we prepared a hot oatmeal breakfast, we became aware of a new problem. We were using much more stove fuel than anticipated. We'd packed four gallons of gas—one gallon per week—but already had used more than a gallon in the first six days. Cooking over a fire was out of the question; it would take us hours to gather enough dwarf willow to prepare a hot meal.

Fortunately, LaRonge Air (our carrier) had told us there was an exploratory mining camp along our route on an unnamed lake about ten miles before Takijak. "They're great guys," said Bill Gawletz, our flight dispatcher, when we had departed. "If you get in trouble, stop!"

Incredible joy! We found apple and blueberry pie, peach cobbler, chocolate cupcakes, fresh coffee, all the candy bars we could eat, and first-class Canadian hospitality at the Kid Creek mining camp. The men at the camp pulled out all the stops to make us feel welcome. We stayed nearly two hours, eating and joking, swapping tales and basking in the warmth of their heated double-walled tent cabin. They had no white gas at the camp, but Don McQuire, the resident helicopter pilot, said he'd fly some in from another camp the next day.

It was 10 P.M. when we reluctantly parted company with our new friends. We planned to paddle on to Takijak Lake that night (about a five-hour trip), make the mile-long portage around the spectacular forty-meter falls above it, and get at least four hours of sleep before we began the northward trek toward the Hood. But by 8 A.M., Takijak was kicking up four-foot rollers. We rejoiced at the discovery of an ice-free passage, but were disappointed that we were wind-bound again.

At 6 P.M., we heard the whirr of a helicopter. It was Don McQuire from Kid Creek camp. He brought us two freshly caught trout, a dozen candy bars, and a gallon of white gas. All we could offer was heartfelt thanks, along with tea and honey.

Within the hour it began to rain. The temperature dropped to 43° and the wind subsided to a constant ten miles per hour—perfect paddling weather! We donned rain suits and gloves, fastened our canoe covers, and headed north into the churning waves. Hour after hour we battled the weather, barely making two miles an hour. When, at 5 A.M., we could take no more, we pitched a hasty camp in a quiet cove and crawled into the wonderful warmth of our sleeping bags. Just before retiring, we medicated ourselves heavily with Yukon Jack and swore to spread the word the moment the fun began.

We all had lost several pounds during the previous two weeks of canoe travel. Our faces and hands were burned raw from the wind and sun, and there were few muscles that didn't ache. A herd of caribou, a few grizzlies, and awesome solitude barely compensated for the abuse to which our bodies had been subjected. Surely, tomorrow would be a better day.

When we arose at 9:30 A.M., the rain had stopped and the persistent north wind had settled to a gentle breeze. We completed the remaining miles across Takijak, and camped at an old Eskimo site in a protected bay. The next morning, we made the mile-and-a-half carry into the connecting lakes that flowed into the Hood River. The skies were clear and the mercury hovered at 83°. There was not a hint of wind to blow away the bugs. Saddled with what seemed to be a never-dwindling load, we slogged light-headed through the swampy tundra, sweat streaming down our bodies. When at last we reached the first lake shore and set down our burdens, we collapsed in wonder and confusion. Was the portage really over or was it just a dream? Marc Hebert drew forth a bottle of peppermint schnaaps and passed it around. A celebration was in order, but no one had the energy to do much more than sip and groan.

Then we saw them—shaggy prehistoric creatures with long

silky hair and menacing curved horns. Musk ox, maybe thirty of them—less than three-hundred yards away! Miraculously, our aches vanished as we grabbed cameras and telephoto lenses, intent on photographing these unusual and rare animals.

For nearly a week thereafter we saw herd after herd of musk ox, which, despite their buffalo size, proved extremely agile. More like mountain goats than cattle, musk ox can turn in a flash and scamper up the steepest hill with surprising speed. Their eyesight and sense of smell is excellent. On several occasions, they spotted us from nearly a mile away! Nevertheless, with care, we could approach them to within a few dozen feet. Once, Reb crawled to within a canoe's length of a large bull. For awhile the animal just stared at him, then he lowered his head, pawed the ground defiantly, and snorted so hard the vapor clouded Reb's glasses. At this, Reb lept up with a scream and raced away from the bull as fast as his legs could carry him, while the equally frightened animal high-tailed it in the opposite direction! When both were about two-hundred yards apart, they simultaneously stopped and looked back. It was quite a show.

The Hood is not a large river, but it is a fast one. The speed of the current varies from a steady three or four miles per hour to nearly ten. Dozens of rapids—large and small—are found along its length, and there are at least three spectacular waterfalls.

To our relief, we were able to run most of the rapids, many of which dropped more than twenty-five feet per mile. But we scouted every pitch and, whenever possible, took the "chicken route" down. When in doubt, we lined or portaged. We were constantly on guard and took the dangers of the river seriously.

Despite our precautions, we all made errors. Reb and Kent swamped when they ran a small ledge without their nylon spray cover; Marc and I became engulfed in man-sized waves in the unyielding hydraulics of a "wrong channel"; and Bob and David Dannert missed a portage and succeeded in running an "unrunnable" rapid. Such are the realities of canoeing in the barren lands.

For a week after we entered the Hood, we enjoyed unseasonably warm weather (temperatures in the 80s) and strong tail winds. The sudden warmth brought forth a new batch of insects, requiring us to don head nets and bug jackets whenever we stopped along the shore.

The upper Hood was shallow, with several miles of punishing rock fans. We pushed and dragged our canoes over the rocks, frequently wading waist deep in the 47° water. Thanks to the unseasonably warm weather this ordinarily unpleasant task was a joy—a nice change from the previous weeks of portaging and fighting head winds.

We paused to fish at the base of nearly every rapid, invariably landing a trout with the first or second cast. The fish were hungry, unsophisticated and bit at any lure. Sometimes, they even competed for the same bait. On one occasion, I caught two fish on the same hook simultaneously! Bob Dannert caught the biggest fish of the trip—a glistening 23-pound lake trout. Everyone used barbless hooks so the big fish could be released without injury.

Once through the rock fans, the Hood became an effortless Huck Finn float. The good current and tail wind allowed us to make six or seven miles per hour without dipping a paddle. We were getting farther and farther ahead of schedule without doing anything. We could complete our required thirteen miles a day in two or three hours.

The result of our efficiency was a real difference of opinion with regard to our plans for the rest of the trip. Some of the crew (myself included) wanted to "bank" miles—to play this uncommonly good weather for all it was worth. We bet the high temperatures and favorable winds couldn't last.

The dissenters reveled in our progress and in the conditions, and saw no reason to push ahead. They wanted to play on the river, not at our pick-up point near the Arctic Ocean.

Fortunately, the crew was mature and experienced—each man an expert in his own right. We discussed the matter intelligently, voted, then kept further thoughts to ourselves. Everyone realized a decision had to be made—and that peace had to be kept.

In the end, the slow-down-and-take-it-easy majority got its way, despite the real concerns expressed by those of us who didn't agree. For the next three days, we just lazed along, pushed by the substantial current and benevolent wind. The work began when we awoke and ended three hours later. It was great while it lasted.

The time of reckoning came on August 11, when the thermometer, which had registered 100° in the sun at noon, began to drop at the rate of ten degrees an hour. By suppertime, the mercury had settled at 37° and the wind had increased to forty miles per hour. At 8 P.M., the rain began, a few drops at first, growing steadily, until it reached thunderstorm proportions.

Whipped by an unyielding forty mile per hour wind, the rain continued without interruption for the next two-and-a-half days. Wind chills approached zero. We cooked, ate, and even relieved ourselves in the vestibules of our tents.

Our canoes were overturned and tied securely to boulders about four feet above the river channel—ordinarily a safe distance. So it came as a real surprise when, twenty-four hours into the storm, Kent discovered they were nearly underwater. He and Bob moved them to higher ground. Twelve hours later, we heard David yell in excited fright, "They're underwater again!" Out of the tents we bolted, filled with disbelief and worry. This time we moved the boats to the top of the esker on which we were camped.

When we finally emerged from our tents on the morning of August 14, we discovered the volume of the river had doubled and its speed tripled! Water poured relentlessly into the channel from every cut in the hillsides, and everywhere there was uprooted, floating plant material. The once-clear waters of the Hood had turned a thick murky brown.

We spoke little as we loaded the boats that morning. Everyone was keenly aware of the dangers. Throughout the channel were huge waves and boiling eddies. The 37° temperature, light rain, and steady head wind of ten miles per hour created ideal conditions for hypothermia. A spill into the river could be fatal. We were two days behind schedule and the only way out was downriver!

The ten-mile paddle to Wilberforce Falls took nearly three hours. We took no chances, paddling within inches of the shoreline whenever possible and lining our canoes around questionable obstacles. Giant waves on the outsides of bends forced us to ferry to the inside every time the river changed directions. Later, we agreed that the frequent stream crossings, which often carried us through waves of monster proportions, were the most dangerous experiences of our trip.

Wilberforce Falls—at 160 feet, the third highest falls in North America—was the highlight of the trip. With an awesome pounding that can be heard for miles, Wilberforce cuts its way through a two-mile red-rock canyon. The three-and-one-half mile portage around it was a grueling all-day affair.

The bad weather had pushed us behind schedule, so we dared not linger. But in celebration of our arrival, we prepared a gourmet supper. We started with a round of hot-buttered rum, followed by a cup of champagne! (Unknown to the rest of the crew, Kent had packed a bottle of bubbly.) Then, freeze-dried steaks, green beans, hash-browned potatoes, and chocolate pudding. Afterward, David and Kent washed the dishes while the rest of us waddled contentedly off to bed.

The skies had cleared by morning, and we were treated to a bright windless day with temperatures in the mid-70s. After a peaceful paddle, we camped that night in the mist of a picturesque falls—our last major obstacle before the polar sea. We had hoped to catch a supper of char here, but the river was too silty for good fishing. Instead, we reluctantly prepared our usual cuisine of soup and Hamburger Helper. Later, we gathered dead dwarf willow branches, and for the first time in four weeks, had a campfire.

We built our fire on a high rock point at the edge of the thundering falls, then sat cross-legged around it, mesmerized by its concentrated warmth and flickering flames. Slowly, a sullenness began to emerge. For nearly a month we had followed a dream, and in just three days, it would be over.

We spent our last two nights at a traditional Inuit char-fishing camp about two miles from the ocean. The Hood was still filthy brown, so we drew clean drinking and cooking water from an isolated pond nearby.

Our original intent was to canoe to the ocean, just to say we'd dipped paddles in Arctic saltwater. But a measure of laziness had set in among the crew; no one wanted to paddle back against the current to our pickup point. Instead, we hiked five miles cross-country to an Inuit fishing camp on Bathurst Inlet and the Arctic Ocean.

Sun-bronzed and wind-burned, our bodies toned by four-hundred miles of canoe travel, we stood confidently on a high wind-blown esker and looked north into the sparkling Arctic sea. Tomorrow, a float plane would carry us to Yellowknife and the comforts of civilization. In three days, we'd be back with our loved ones and friends. There'd be bills to pay, lawns to mow and cars to wash. In unison, we burst out laughing. What crazy ways the white man has, we agreed. We had come to envy the world of the Inuit—an appreciation our families and friends would never understand.

BACKWHAT?!

We Know How To Backferry!

FIRST, LET ME MAKE IT PERFECTLY clear that I am not a risk taker. I wouldn't bet two bucks on the Minnesota lottery or waste a 29-cent stamp to enter a publisher's sweepstakes. On the other hand, betting on a sure thing is a challenge I can't resist, even when, to the untrained eye, the window of success appears marginally small.

It began quite innocently during an unexpected October snowfall. The previous three weeks had been marked by Indian summer days with temperatures in the sixties, so friends and I figured we could sneak in four days of canoeing in the Boundary Waters before we waxed our skis. But the night before we were to leave, the blizzard struck and our canoeing plans were dashed to the winds.

I poured myself some hot chocolate, threw another log in the stove and watched it snow. Then, determined to drown out what was with what I wanted, I spent the evening scanning old canoeing and camping magazines. An article about canoeing with kids caught my eye, and I methodically browsed through it. Along with the usual equipment recommendations was a proven list of "do's and don'ts"—one recommendation of which was a firm admonition that teenagers should not be allowed to run rapids. The only exception was for "highly trained crews in capable whitewater canoes." I wondered exactly what the author meant by "highly trained" and "capable whitewater canoes" so, with time to kill, I phoned some whitewater instructors and posed the question that had been bothering me for months:

"Do you think a group of fifteen- and sixteen-year-olds who've never paddled a canoe before could learn enough from a good teacher in four or five practice sessions to do a remote Canadian river that has long stretches of Class II and III rapids?"

An international classification scale grades rapids from I (riffles) to VI (you possess a significant death wish). Class III is considered "difficult" and is characterized by small falls and three- to four-foot waves. Expert maneuvering and route-finding skills are necessary.

The answer was unanimous: No Way! The response was more adamant when the consultants learned I was thinking of using stock Grumman Eagle and Old Town Discovery canoes.

But here was a challenge I couldn't refuse! I had taught teenagers canoeing for fifteen years and knew that good training would spell success. Kids learn fast—actually, much faster than most adults. The problem is getting them to pay attention. But once committed, they're on a roll and you'd need a snowplow to stop them. In the past, I'd led teen crews down the relatively placid English, Steel and Kopka Rivers in northern Ontario. It was time to move on to a tough whitewater run. Admittedly, our Discoveries and deep-keeled Grummans were ill-suited to the demands of a rapid-filled river, where quick turns are essential. But with skill and caution, we'd get them through. I had always believed that skills were more important than equipment. Here was my chance to prove it.

For nearly twenty years, I'd been eyeing a small river called the Gull, which emptied into Ontario's Lake Nipigon. Research indicated that the remote sixty-mile route was virtually untraveled. Rapids rated Class II and III and beyond—and portages (where they existed) were unmaintained and difficult to find.

The Ontario trip guide was emphatic: "This river is not at all easy to travel. The rapids are very long and the portages are overgrown and difficult to find. It is definitely not a route for the inexperienced canoeist!"

My maps suggested there were more than thirty sets of rapids and two major falls along the river. The average drop in the upper section was more than twenty-five feet per mile. Acquaintances who had run the river said the calm stretches moved along at more than five miles an hour. (Most lazy local streams drop two to three feet per mile. Ten feet per mile is considered whitewater; fifteen to twenty feet per mile is usually about the limit for open canoes.) One veteran Minnesota camp Widgiwagen guide who had paddled the Thelon and Back Rivers in the Northwest Territories said that she was intimidated by this river. "Too fast . . . no eddies . . . no chance for error. It's beautiful but frightening. I don't think I'd do it again," she said. When I told her of my plan to lead a crew of teens down the river, she politely told me I was crazy.

So I contacted Mattie McNair, who, with her husband Paul Landry, had authored the revised edition of *Basic River Canoeing*—one of the definitive whitewater technique books. Mattie and Paul directed the Canadian Outward Bound Camp and regularly paddled the Gull River. I trusted their judgment. If Paul and Mattie gave me two thumbs down, I'd revise my hypothesis and search for a less-technical river.

Mattie came right to the point in a letter: "It's a tough run, and many portages are a must. There's no portaging the mile-long section around the burn, which rates Class III at the top." She then offered advice on specific rapids and enclosed a hand-drawn map of the river that detailed every major obstacle. Things were looking up: She hadn't said "no way."

The magic words came to mind again: "Skill" and "Caution"— and for my part, "Research, research and more research!"

Remarkably, the trip filled within days after it was advertised. Colleague Al Todnem and I would share the leadership. Tom Schwinghamer, an experienced physician and Sherry Akins— teacher and mother of one of the participants, would go along for the ride. The final count was twelve—four boys, four girls and four adults. Al and Doc had done several backwoods trips with me and knew the ropes, but the others were as green as the paint on my Old Town canoe. Their canoeing education would have to begin at once.

First, we went over the essential forms and equipment lists. There would be no second chances on the Gull, I told my charges, so personal gear must reflect the challenge. There was no room for blue jeans and plastic rain suits, or for bulky sleeping bags that consumed half a pack. Surplus military woolens, discount-store acrylics, polypropylene and nylon were the rule. Every kid had his own list and I carefully checked off the items as they appeared.

The canoes were my responsibility. I outfitted them with thickly padded curved wood yokes that were built to fit teen shoulders, then added a canvas tumpline to further ease the burden. Thick, non-slip knee pads were glued to the floor of every canoe. Twenty-foot-long polypropylene tracking lines were installed at cutwater, then meticulously coiled and secured under loops of shock cord on the decks. Loops of parachute cord threaded through holes drilled in the gunnels provided anchor points to tie in packs. Every boat was numbered, named, and assigned to the crew responsible for it. Participants were required to memorize a list of operational rules before they were cleared to paddle. Absolutely nothing was left to chance.

Every week before the trip, there was homework, and the admonition that "If you don't do it, you don't go!" I was a hard taskmaster who expected perfection. Everyone was required to study selected pages from canoeing literature. There were lectures and instructional handouts on paddling techniques, ferrying, hypothermia, wilderness first aid and safety. I showed an instructional film at nearly every meeting. Every action in the movie was analyzed and reanalyzed as canoe partners lined up, paddles in hand, and dry-practiced what they saw on the screen. Sometimes, I even gave tests on what they had learned. A passing grade was not good enough. Everyone had to earn a perfect score!

There were also a number of "special projects." Some kids sewed nylon stuff sacks for food and equipment, while others dehydrated food or made trail bars and "monster" cookies. We taught classes on waterproofed packing, map interpretation, physical conditioning, hygiene, hypothermia and water purification. Every youngster got a thorough backwoods education before the wheels rolled north.

On-the-water training began with two half-day sessions of maneuvering on a quiet pond. To eliminate confusion, each youngster decided at the outset which end of the canoe he or she would paddle on the trip. Switching ends was not permitted. Students were required to master the four crucial paddling strokes for their positions in the canoe. With these, they could do all the maneuvers needed to avoid obstacles; canoes could be side-slipped right or left, smartly pivoted around obstacles, and stabilized when crossing eddy lines. There are other important maneuvers, but experience suggested it was best to keep things simple.

After eight hours of practicing side-slips, pivots and back-paddling, the crew was ready to canoe in currents. I chose a local stream that had easy riffles and a strong flow, but no dangerous rapids. Here, we could safely practice eddy turns and ferries without the dangers of the hydraulics that accompany big waves. Hour after hour we ferried and turned, ferried and turned. By day's end, the message was clear and the seed had taken hold. Next week, we'd move on to a big river with "real" rapids!

A spring Saturday found us on Minnesota's lower Snake River—an easy whitewater run when water levels are moderate. But friend Darrell Foss and I stood at the river's edge that cold gray morning and stared in disbelief at the three-foot-high rollers that crashed against the bridge pilings. I set my thermometer into the water. The mercury settled at 48 degrees. Current speed? At least ten miles an hour! This was no place for an inexperienced crew!

For awhile, we considered aborting the paddle, but we had driven two hours to get here and it was our last training trip. The Gull would have waves like this; better that the kids should learn to control their boats in them now. We had intended to practice eddy turns and side-slip maneuvers but the huge waves made this impossible. "We'll practice backferries today," I said cheerfully. "If you can ferry in this stuff, you'll have no trouble on the Gull."

I set the example, and the kids followed suit. When the river turned, we angled our sterns smartly toward the inside bend and vigorously backpaddled. The backferry took hold almost immediately and the canoes danced sideways across the river, with no downstream slip. Too bad we were alone on the river and there were no onlookers to impress.

Then, around a bend, we drifted by a red Coleman canoe with two men aboard who were not wearing life jackets. A case of beer and mound of personal gear weighted the craft to dangerously low freeboard. We dutifully exchanged waves then parted positions on the river—our canoes for the inside bend, theirs for the outside flow. "Ferry right, herd 'em over!" I commanded. The men in the Coleman gaped at our near broadside approach to the rough water.

"You kids need help? You're s'posed to take 'em right down the middle!" they called. There was no reason to answer. They wouldn't understand.

The Coleman powered around the bend while we ferried into an eddy, then put ashore for lunch. A half hour later, we were back on the river, cautiously bumping our way down the shoreline. "Look there," I pointed. "See how those waves are piling up on the outside curve? Good thing you guys can ferry or you'd be part of that debris."

At this, one of the kids said, "Hey Cliff, what's that red thing over there?" I squinted through my bifocals. Damned if it wasn't the Coleman canoe that had passed us earlier. It was solidly wrapped around the huge sweeper we had been eyeing with concern. There was no sign of the paddlers. I remembered they had not worn life jackets and feared they might have drowned.

Very cautiously, we ferried around the bend and made for an eddy where we could view the entire scene. The canoe had been swept into the tree, where it swamped and jackknifed. Were the men trapped in the debris? I pulled out my binoculars and searched the pounding water for a splash of color—anything that might provide hope. Nothing. A hush fell upon the group as each one of us said a silent prayer. The huge waves, the giant brush pile, the half submerged canoe—it would be a miracle if either man had gotten out alive.

The kids were unusually quiet for the duration of the run. In unison, and without showing emotion, they followed me, duplicating with military precision every movement of my canoe. I valued their trust and prayed I wouldn't screw up.

Two hours later we reached our take-out point on the St. Croix River, and I breathed a huge sigh of relief. As we pulled the canoes up the gravel beach, a state trooper appeared and asked if we'd seen a red canoe upstream. "Yeah," I answered. "Wrapped around a tree about five miles back."

"Those guys were scared white when I picked them up. Said a bunch of inexperienced kids were on the river and they were sure to drown. Said you guys couldn't even paddle your boats straight, without crashing the shore. They said I should get here fast, maybe get a jet boat and go upstream to help."

"No sweat," said Bruce, our crew clown. "We know how to backferry!" "Back what?" asked the officer. "Forget it," said Bruce. "We know how to paddle!"

And they certainly did! In June, 1986, our crew of eight teenagers and four adults canoed the Gull River without incident. The river was as tough as we'd heard, but no one swamped or even scraped a rock. Whenever dancing horsetails loomed ahead, the kids would immediately reverse power and go into "backferry position." It was a proud sight.

The Diablo Lake Portage

IT BEGAN IN 1974, when friends Bob Brown, Darrell Foss and I decided to build wood-strip solo canoes. I constructed the Minnesota Canoe Association fourteen-footer and Darrell followed suit with a similarily styled boat of his own design. Brownie, a free spirit in these matters, built up a tippy freestyle canoe that he lovingly named Itty Bit. On her baptism, Itty Bit promptly dumped Bob into a backwater of the Mississippi River, upon which, Darrell and I re-christened her Tender Bit.

The idea was to field-test the three divergent designs in an untamed wilderness environment. At trip's end, the best boat would earn for its owner all the beers he could drink.

After studying dozens of routes, we settled on the Steel River in northern Ontario. It had everything we could ask for—thin, shallow streams and beaver ponds, testy rapids, picturesque waterfalls, a twenty-five-mile lake, and a two-mile mega-portage (at the very start!) over chest-high boulders that gained four-hundred feet of elevation in the first half mile. We agreed the Steel would provide a perfect test for our new solo canoes.

Our first stop was Terrace Bay, where cafe owner D.E. Miller had agreed to shuttle our vehicle to trip's end.

"That Diablo Lake portage (the two-miler) will kill ya," professed Miller as he scrutinized my topographic map. Then, he grinned broadly and suggested an alternate route—a two-lane highway, he called it—built by a youth works program years ago. "Hardly anyone knows about it," he winked.

I studied the map. It was five, maybe six miles long—three times farther than the commonly recommended Diablo portage. "I dunno, looks awfully long. Are you sure it's better?" I questioned.

Miller faced me squarely, "Hell, I live here, don't I?"

With that, I shut my mouth and suggested to my friends that we "trust the locals."

A three-minute drive from the restaurant brought us to the "two-lane highway," which was barely wide enough for our solo canoes. It was a network of tangled brush, downed trees and knee-high boulders. It would cross two lakes and several creeks and ponds before it terminated at Diablo Lake, at the end of which was another killer portage.

We shouldered our canoes and began the long, gentle ascent of the first hill. Seven hours later we came to the first lake, where we encountered a man and his son with an eighty-pound Chestnut canoe. They had begun the carry the day before! Smug smiles flashed briefly. We were beginning to appreciate the joy of light-weight solo canoes.

For twenty minutes we splashed and played in the cool, clear water, refilled canteens and formulated a strategy for the next leg of our journey—a gentle uphill trek of about two miles through thick brush and downed trees. Until now, we'd been double-packing the portage in half-mile stretches, first carrying the heaviest pack, paddles and camera, then returning for the canoe and remaining gear. The method seemed prudent, given the uncertainty of the trail and the ninety-degree heat. But it was terribly slow—we were making much less than a mile an hour. It was already 6 P.M., the sun was almost down and there was no place to camp. To save time, we decided to carry everything at once—a back-killing load of around a hundred pounds per man.

Two more hours of portaging brought us to Fishnet Lake—a mile from our ultimate destination—where sweat-stained and too tired to go on, we searched for a habitable campsite. Nothing! Ultimately, we roughed out a tent spot on an incline and tied our canoes to trees to keep them from sliding into the lake. It was dead calm and 94°. Hordes of black flies suddenly appeared, and it began to rain. We ate a hasty supper of freeze-dried chili, and in minutes, we were fast asleep.

We awoke to light rain and the same scenario as the day before. We horsed our boats through thickets, snaked them between trees, hopped from rock to rock, and sweltered in the hundred-degree heat. Occasionally, there were patches of murky water to paddle, and some fresh water to fill our canteens. But mostly there were portages.

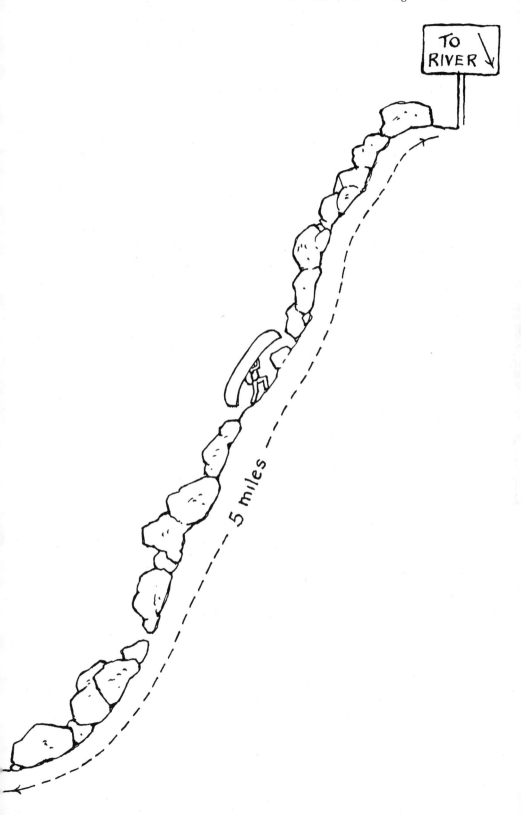

We now talked openly about aborting the trip. But how? The unknown was preferable to going back over that God-forsaken trail. We passed our bottle of peppermint schnaaps around again and again and cursed D.E. Miller. We'd had it!

At 3 P.M. on the second day, we nosed our canoes into the quiet bay that marked the start of the true paddling—twelve-mile-long Cairngorm Lake, our first real water. We lunched on a lichen-splached outcrop, swam and drank the cool, clear water. We sipped eagerly from our store of liquor and toasted our little boats. We'd endured sweltering heat, black flies, persistent rain and eighteen hours of grueling portages to get here. Was it worth it? "Absolutely not!" we agreed. But, "Thank God for little boats," we chorused, agreeing that we each had built the best canoe. And then we passed the schnaaps bottle around again!

Darrell Foss and I make an annual solo canoe trip to the Boundary Waters Canoe Area in late October, when the people and bugs are gone. Friend Chic Sheridan eagerly joined us for these outings until he fell victim to Lou Gehrig's disease and passed away in 1986. Bob Brown ultimately discovered he hates camping out, and now limits his canoe trips to day ventures on local waterways or goes to places that have Holiday Inns nearby. Bob has designed a number of wonderful solo and tandem canoes for a number of canoe companies. My favorite solo canoe—a fif-teen-foot, four-inch Bell Traveler, was designed by Bob at my insistence.

Kosdaw the Troublemaker

FOR MORE THAN A MILE, we've been intimidated by the awesome roar of Manitou Falls—the spot where, according to Chippewa legend, the 100-yard-wide Fond du Lac River disappears into a hole in the ground.

We run a small ledge, paddle a short section of foot-high haystacks, and slip into a quiet eddy about two-hundred yards above the cascade. We pull the canoes well up on shore, tie them securely, and struggle through dense undergrowth and burned timber to a high, lonely rock overlook. Below us is Manitou Falls.

Darrell Foss runs his finger methodically along the line that marks the river on the map, searching for the portage. The canyon wall to the north of the falls stretches upward some two-hundred forty feet, but to the west, it rises only sixty feet.

Carefully, using binoculars, we search for signs of a portage, but none is visible. Dancing horsetails leap from the falls dozens of feet into the air and a penetrating mist hovers cloud-like above the pounding water. Sure enough, it appears that the Fond du Lac does disappear into the ground!

But our maps and trip notes tell the truth: A portion of the river does drops below ground for perhaps fifty feet, while a second channel bends 90 degrees to the left, turning right again in a few dozen feet. The result is a spectacular view, and from our vantage point, a frightening one. No wonder the Indians call this the "Fall of the Great Spirit."

"The portage begins here in this bay," Darrell says finally, "just at the head of the falls."

The "just at the head of the falls" part evokes an eerie silence from the group but there is no outward indication of fear. "We'll follow you to the portage, Cliff," Jerry Smith says sarcastically. "Whistle if you have problems!"

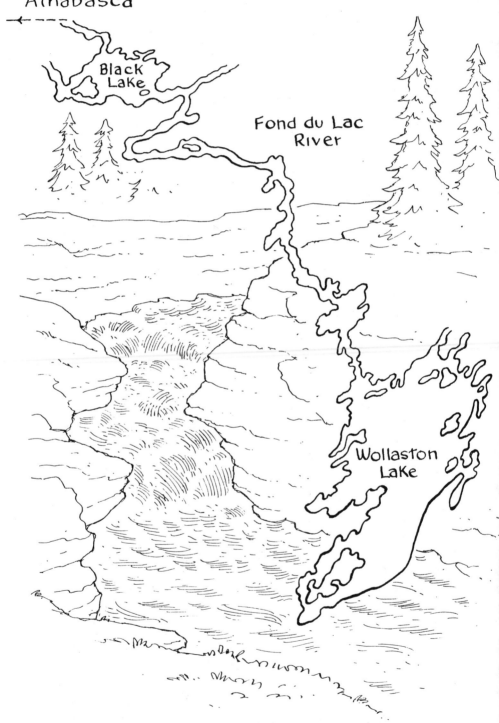

To Lake
Athabasca

Black
Lake

Fond du Lac
River

Wollaston
Lake

"Sure, " I mutter, then the four of us scramble apprehensively down the sandstone bluff to the waiting canoes. After a few moments of silent paddling, we reach the portage and pause to take in one of the most beautiful views of our trip—the great falls of the Fond du Lac.

The Fond du Lac is hardly an undiscovered river. However, getting to and from to the waterway is so difficult that the integrity of the area's remoteness is guaranteed. Perhaps a half-dozen parties canoe the river in a season. Geographically, the Fond du Lac begins in the northwest tip of Saskatchewan at Wollaston Lake. It finishes in a burst of speed at Stony Rapids on Lake Athabasca, about fifty miles below the border of the Northwest Territories.

I discovered the Fond du Lac by accident while reading Nick Nickel's book *Canoe Canada*. Nick called the route "A remote challenging river for expert whitewater canoeists." This description, plus the river's total length of two-hundred miles, suggested we might complete the run—including the three-thousand road miles—in fourteen to seventeen days. A recently completed tote road to Wollaston Lake would enable us to drive to the put-in, thus saving hundreds of dollars in charter float plane costs. The die was cast and we began our research, planning to canoe the river in August 1979.

First on our list of required readings was Sigurd Olson's book *Runes of the North*. In a chapter entitled *Fond du Lac,* Olson detailed his experiences on the river. But Olson's remembrances of the Fond du Lac turned out to be nothing like what we encountered. He experienced the river as a mass of protruding rocks and shallow, drought-choked channels. We saw it swollen by weeks of unrelenting rain and filled with powerful waves and uncompromising souse holes. As every canoeist will attest, water levels make a profound difference in the experience!

We then sent personal letters to Eric Morse, Sigurd Olson and Professor Bert Hamilton of Queens University, all of whom paddled the route. From Olson came a letter of encouragement: "The trip is exceptionally beautiful, very worthwhile." From Morse and Hamilton came detailed notes of their expedition two decades earlier.

Our next stop was the Minnesota Historical Society, where we obtained copies of the 1796 narrative of David Thompson and the 1892 diary of Joseph B. Tyrrell, one of Canada's most famous explorers. Thompson, a well known geographer, explorer and British astronomer, was first to document the Fond du Lac—only he went backward, upstream from Stony Rapids to Wollaston. Essentially, Thompson was looking for a fur-trade route into the Churchill River—one that would bypass the tortuous thirteen-mile Methe (La Loche) portage. The idea was to bring fur-trade canoes across Lake Athabasca, up the Fond du Lac River, down Wollaston and Reindeer Lakes, and into the Churchill watershed near the Frog Portage. But Thompson's journey was so fraught with trouble that only one official British expedition followed, that of J.B. Tyrrell in 1892. Information from both accounts suggested that the Fond du Lac was more than just a remote exciting white-water run; it was a unique part of the North American fur-trade history.

A study of the map indicated that the most difficult parts of our journey would be the thiry-mile open-water traverse of Wollaston Lake, the twenty-mile southwesterly crossing of island-barren Black Lake, and the five miles of portaging around Elizabeth Falls and Woodcock Rapids, which would take us from Black Lake to Stony Rapids. Little did we realize at the time that our most formidable obstacle would be the road to Wollaston itself.

Our traveling outfit consisted of a 1977 Jeep Wagoneer with a loaded trailer and two Old Town Tripper canoes tied to overhead racks. The Jeep, we discovered, was a good choice, for it's doubtful that an ordinary car would have survived the 523 miles (round trip) of road north of LaRonge.

Essentially, Canadian Highway 105 was built as a tote road from Missinipe to the uranium mine near Rabbit Lake, west of Wollaston. Though the road is graded frequently, large rocks in the roadway and flying stones are commonplace. And the black sticky oil used to cement road dust adheres to everything. The Saskatchewan Highway Department has jokingly posted eighty kmph (fifty miles per hour) maximum speed signs and "Slow down, save your windshield" warnings within yards of one another!

The last two-hundred miles of gravel are announced by a sign that says, "Warning: Next 322 km travel at your own risk: No services, no assistance!" During the ride, we broke a trailer spring, shredded a trailer tire and lost a five-gallon Jerry can from its mounting bracket. The road dust was so bad that we sealed all the crevices in the Jeep with duct tape. Trucks of three tons or more, and four-wheel drive vehicles like our own, were the only vehicles we encountered along the way.

Much of the road is built over muskeg, so road conditions continue to be unpredictable. For example, when I last drove the tote road in 1990, my Chevy van incurred $500 worth of stone damage and a cracked windshield. The drive to Wollaston, we discovered, was but a preview of some of the unusual happenings that were to come.

It was overcast on the morning of departure from Wollaston Lake, and there was a very strong northwest wind. Our original intent was to paddle the entire thirty-mile shoreline of the lake to the mouth of the river that day, but as the wind grew in intensity, we knew we'd be lucky to get out of the bay. To allow for more time on the river, we decided to hire a Wollaston Lodge-owned motorboat to take us to the headwaters of the Fond du Lac.

The young college student from Toronto who was to take us across supposedly knew the lake blindfolded.

"Ever tow canoes before?" I asked.

"Nope," he grinned, apparently certain there would be no problems.

"The idea is to keep the canoes trailing dead center in the wake," I instructed. "If you speed up too fast or turn too quick, a canoe could fall off the wave line and swamp. If that happens, it could be torn in half, maybe even yank the transom right off your boat!"

"We'll get you there, aye mate," he drawled confidently.

I tied the two canoes in tandem to a harness on the transom of the powerboat, climbed aboard and gave the "go" sign. The kid turned the boat into the waist-high waves, punched the throttle, and instantly swamped the lead canoe. "Thank God we're still in the bay!" I screamed.

Fortunately, there was no damage and we were able to salvage both the canoe and everything in it. I was ready to abort the mission, but the kid wanted to try again and my crew was chomping at the bit.

"Okay, just slow down next time!" I admonished.

Within minutes we were waterborne again, skimming northward at half speed. Casually, I looked at my map, then nudged my friend beside me. "Look here, Darrell, this guy's going too far east, don't you think?"

"C'mon, Cliff, he's the guide!"

"Yeah, okay."

With that, I folded my map contentedly and watched the scenery pass. Two hours later, I heard a coughing sound that suggested we were out of gas. No problem. Our guide shut down the twin engines, and plugged in the second of three tanks. Then he withdrew a tiny Xeroxed copy of a map of the area, and squinted at it.

"Any of you guys know where we are?" he said sheepishly.

I looked at my friends and together we burst out laughing. Our guide was lost!

I pulled out my compass and map and ultimately determined that we were about five miles off course. "Head thataway," I said, pointing west toward the Fond du Lac River.

It was 37°, nearly dark, and raining when we arrived at the lake outlet and our jump-off point. The motor coughed again and our guide plugged in the remaining five-gallon gas tank—a questionable fuel supply for the thirty-mile return run. The waves were as large as before and the rain was turning to ice. The man had a light plastic rain jacket, but no hat or gloves.

"Weather's gettin' bad; maybe you better camp here with us tonight," I offered.

"Nyah, I can make it," he called confidently.

With that, he fired up an engine and turned south with the running waves. When we returned to Wollaston Lake Lodge two weeks later, we learned that miraculously, he did not run out of gas or die of hypothermia.

We camped that first night just east of Hatchet Lake at a well-used Indian caribou hunting camp. Scattered about are parts of caribou antler, pieces of hide, tin cans and a profusion of LaBatt's Blue beer bottles. The remains of a stove-equipped tepee and wooden toboggan occupy the west end of our camp site. Several red-painted drums of aviation fuel lay along the shoreline. We drop to sleep amidst the drone of mosquitoes. Tomorrow, we agree, will bring a better day.

In the morning, we battle a strong north wind across Hatchet Lake, then pause at the outlet to chat with a Chippewa Indian who is fishing for grayling. I ask him about the rapids and portages ahead, but he speaks no English and just smiles politely.

Running the rapids out of Hatchet Lake is interesting, in that we have to pivot around a mid-stream boulder and get the canoe into a narrow slot scarcely a paddle width's distance from shore—this amidst overhanging vegetation. It is an exhilarating ride, the water clear and white with dancing horsetails. Our feelings of the Fond du Lac begin to improve!

Back at Wollaston Lake, the native Canadians had told us that because of intensive uranium exploration in the area, we wouldn't see much wildlife. So it is surprising to see all sorts of animals. Within the first week, we observe a moose (within fifty feet), as well as black bear, wolverine and snowy owl. A fish for every three casts is the rule, not the exception. Each night we fill ourselves with walleye, northern pike and shimmering grayling. After two weeks, our food pack is scarcely lighter than the day it was packed.

Our Saskatchewan Department of Tourism trip guide is developing an unfortunate habit of making the difficult rapids sound easy and the easy ones sound hard. So it is with Thompson Rapids. The rapid itself is perhaps a half-mile long, broken into two parts—the first part running through a high rock canyon. The guide suggests the rapid may be run far right, but it neglects to mention the four-foot high engulfing wave and subsequent two-foot ledge below.

We study the portage from the right bank.

"Let's line it," suggests Dan Rooney.

I hesitate, then point to a large boulder about six feet from shore, "Somehow, we've got to get the boat around that."

Darrell—the most level-headed member of our group—says he'd rather portage.

Mulling it over, I suggest Danny and I run it in our covered canoe. "Maybe station Jerry and Darrell at the base of the pitch with rescue lines."

"Yeah, okay, it's your boat, Cliff," Darrell says. I pause.

"All right, you guys," I say, "Let's portage!"

Near the base of the rapid is a large ledge, in all likelihood the one reported by Thompson in his 1796 narrative. We reconstruct the tragedy we'd read about before our trip:

There, on July 9, 1796, was David Thompson, sitting in the middle of his birch-bark canoe, fending off the bank with his paddle while his two Indian companions, Paddy and Kosdaw, line the canoe up around the ledge. Unwittingly, the Indians let the bow of the canoe get out too far in the current and the craft begins to broach. Thompson yells, "Let go the line," but there is no response. Without delay, he draws a folding knife from his pocket and cuts the rope; the canoe plummets headlong over the falls and capsizes in the rapid below. Miraculously, Thompson makes his way to the sandy beach at the base of the rapid, his foot badly cut.

According to Thompson's diary, he lost everything except his pocket knife, a tent of gray cotton, a pewter basin, his gun and an axe.

For several days Thompson and his Indian friends live off berries, until they find an eagle's nest. Kosdaw climbs the nest and throws the young eaglets to the ground. The men cook and eat the birds, but later Thompson and Paddy become violently ill with amoebic dysentery. It is then that Kosdaw informs his companions that the yellow fat from the young birds, which they (not Kosdaw) had eaten, is poisonous.

"Why didn't you tell us the eagle fat was poisonous?" asks Thompson.

"You didn't ask," answers Kosdaw, who suddenly bursts into tears.

Fearing that Thompson might die and be revenged by other white men, Kosdaw pleads with the leader to give him a "writing" that will absolve him of guilt. Though sickened and weak, Thompson writes a brief account of the poisoning on birch bark. Days later, the three men are rescued by a wandering band of Chippewas.

As we stand at the base of Thompson Rapids, we wonder if it is Kosdaw who had brought trouble to our party some twenty miles upstream at the lake that bears his name.

It was early evening and we'd just completed a nice three-quarter mile run through a bouncy rapid. In the pool below the rapid, near the mouth of Kosdaw Lake, we spotted an ideal campsite. The picturesque spot overlooked a protected bay, perched on a high point with a broad, sloping rock face. There were plenty of trees, and a nice breeze to blow away the bugs.

Our camp set, we turned to the evening meal—freeze-dried Chili Mac with a side order of chicken soup and salted nut rolls. "Dinner!" I called when all was ready. And in she came, four-hundred pounds of healthy looking black bear. She showed no fear. Neither did we.

We all had encountered enough bears back home in Minnesota to know how to deal with this one. Or so we thought. We whistled, banged on pots, yelled. But she came still closer. We chased her into the bush, but she retreated only momentarily. Then Jerry smacked her solidly in the rump with a large rock. That did it. She woofed and bared her teeth, then came charging out at Danny, who, white-faced, dashed into the lake.

Hurriedly we grabbed everything—food, packs, tents, clothes—and threw it into the canoes. In a second the canoes were launched, and we were on our way. The bear stood her ground, teeth bared, snarling, unreceptive to the braying of her cubs in the woods. Our hearts pounding, we paddled off in search of another campsite. Defiantly, she followed us around the point, still woofing and clacking her teeth. I'm convinced she'd have had us for dinner if we'd gone ashore again.

The sun was still above the horizon at 10 P.M. when we left the bear site. For three hours we scouted Kosdaw Lake in search of a camp spot. Nothing. The land around the lake was all swamp. Even in an emergency, a site could not be hacked from the wilderness. Then, the sky clouded over, producing the first real darkness we had known on the trip.

There we were, at 1:30 A.M., paddling about with compass and flashlight in search of a campsite. Finally, we came to a high knoll. We built a fire atop the knoll and dragged the canoes up the hillside. There was barely room for a single tent, so we all crowded in together in the big Eureka! Timberline tent. In the night it rained, and in the morning the wind came up again, more fiercely than before. Kosdaw was making big trouble!

As the Fond du Lac proceeds west from Thompson Rapids to Manitou Falls, it takes on new character. This is canyon country. Spectacular sandstone rock cliffs reach upward more than 200 feet. There are a number of short, significant rapids in this section, but nearly all are canoeable.

Beyond Manitou Falls, the river narrows. Long stretches (up to two miles) of moderate rapids prevail. We stop to scout Brink Rapids; we line two ledges and run the rest. But Brassy Rapids, a two-mile long rock garden, is sheer joy. We break the rule about scouting and finish the run in fifteen minutes. At the lake below Brassy, we look for a camp site.

The temperature drops to 38°, and a cold rain sets in. We build a warming fire under our rain tarp and sip hot chocolate spiced with peppermint schnaaps to dull the cold. Then, in the distance, we hear the drone of an engine. The noise gets louder, then above the trees a float-equipped Beaver appears. The plane circles, cuts power, and settles down onto the lake. The Beaver chugs over to our camp and stops a few feet from shore.

A tall, unshaven man in his mid-30s emerges smiling from the cockpit, and steps out on one pontoon. He introduces himself as Brian Dayton, a uranium mining engineer, and tells us that his uranium exploration crew will be arriving at our location shortly by helicopter. We stand dumbfounded at this invasion of our privacy.

In an hour the chopper, flown by a 21-year-old New Zealander, sets down. Two Chippewa Indians and a variety of foodstuffs, beer and camping gear emerge from the aircraft. The crew is friendly and offers us fresh pork chops, mushrooms, onions, cauliflower and green peppers, which we gladly accept. I make Oriental stir fry for everyone on my gasoline stove. The eight of us consume two cases of LaBatt's Blue, and in the process solve all the world's problems. The invasion is a friendly one.

Staring into the flickering fire, we discuss the impact of uranium mining upon the area. Ironically, Brian and the young chopper pilot are opposed to the exploration but view it as inevitable. Brian is determined to damage the bush as little as possible. The Indians unload two galvanized garbage cans from the chopper. "We leave a clean camp," says Brian. "The trash you see up here comes mostly from fly-in fishermen." Americans? I wondered.

(Fortunately, the mining engineers found nothing of value along the Fond du Lac. Except for some graffiti on a lichen-splashed outcrop near Black Lake, the river is wilder now than it was in 1979.)

In the morning we say our good-byes and head west to Black Lake, the next leg of our journey.

Twelve miles wide, Black Lake stretches forty miles to the southwest. Only one large island and a handful of tiny ones break the fierce northwest wind. We camp at the mouth of the lake on a beautiful sand beach, prepare a supper of freeze-dried spaghetti and snack'n cake and set our mental alarm clocks for 3 A.M. We must paddle the twenty miles on Black Lake in the early morning hours before the wind comes up.

At 3:20 A.M. I sluggishly push aside the tent flap and peer into the harsh grayness of the night. The temperature hovers at 38°, and to the south the sky is black. The wind, no less violent than the day before, blows steadily from the north. We debate. Should we go, or remain wind-bound here for the day? As trip leader, I reluctantly make the decision. We go!

Within the hour we're riding the waves, wind in our faces. We cut off a large bay, which puts us more than a mile from shore. The wind worsens; water splashes into the Old Towns. I'm grateful for my splash cover, but the second boat has none. Darrell and Jerry are taking on water, so we angle toward shore. But the water gets no rougher so we continue, and six hours later we arrive at Camp Grayling (a fly-in fishing resort), where we radio-telephone Stony Rapids to verify our flight on the two Cessna 185s that we'd booked in advance. "Sorry," says the voice on the phone, "We can't honor our commitment. DOT (Department of Transportation) regulations now make it illegal to carry canoes longer than sixteen feet on Cessna 185s."

Drat! Our canoes are seventeen-footers. Kosdaw again! Then, the voice on the phone says, "We've got a Twin Otter gassed and ready to go. He'll be in the Territories for the next few days, so if you boys want to fly, you'd better do it now." Silence. We check our billfolds. The flight is much more expensive than anticipated, but we have no choice. "Okay," I say reluctantly, "Let's fly."

Thirty minutes later, the turbo-prop Twin arrives. On board, the pilot tells us there's a major storm to the north. "There's snow above Athabasca," he reports. The outside air temperature indicator on takeoff reads 34°. It's a great day for going home.

River Angel

IT'S EARLY JUNE on a wild Canadian river I've paddled five times before. High water, low water, or in-between—no matter; I know every curve and obstacle by heart. There are no surprises, or so I think.

Round the bend I see the dancing horsetails of the rapid. A straightforward s-curve at any water level, I know just where to run it. A crossdraw at the bow, followed by a stern pry, sets up the turn. Deep down, pangs of conscience tell me to check the pitch from shore before I run it. But I arrogantly dismiss the mental warning and plunge confidently ahead.

Beyond the shallows are the two rocks that mark the vee of the safe water course. We're on automatic pilot now—just follow the run-out to the bottom, turn right, and we're home free.

Then we see it—a half-submerged sapling that blocks the way. "Back!" I scream. But it is too late. The canoe spins suddenly sideways, swamps and overturns. The water is barely two feet deep but there is enough power in the determined current to wrap the golden Kevlar hull tightly around a mid-stream boulder. The muffled cracking sound I hear indicates the craft is breaking up. Safe on shore, my partner and I helplessly watch the destruction.

Seconds later it is over, and we begin the painful process of extracting the remains of my once-beautiful canoe from the clutches of the rock. Fortunately, the craft is intact, though hours of repair work lie ahead. The pride of my fleet is now a "working" boat.

I don't have to search for the right words to describe the experience. "Stupid" comes immediately to mind, and it sticks. After all, even a well-read novice knows better than to run a rapid without first checking it. I could blame my bow partner; some stern paddlers do. But it is my fault. I know it's my fault!

Ironically, I was warned about the dangers of this drop the moment I saw the plumes of dancing water. Deep in my subconscious, I had heard the gentle voice of my river angel. "Put ashore and check this rapid," she had whispered softly. But I had turned deaf ears and thrown caution to the wind.

It happened again that summer, on another Canadian river I'd paddled three times before. The "always canoeable" Class III rapid was etched clearly in my mind: Begin far right, clear the narrow chute below, then pivot quickly upstream and ferry across to river left. Just before crashing the bank, turn down-current and catch the yard-wide slot near shore. High water makes the run easier, but it can be done if there is any downstream flow.

Still smarting from the hurt of wrapping my golden canoe a month earlier, I decided to walk the right bank and check for obstacles in the ferry path. There were none. However, to see the negotiable slot on river left, I'd have to ferry across river, disembark, then walk two-hundred yards on precarious boulders. Why mess around for thirty minutes to ascertain what I already knew? Hadn't I faithfully walked the right shore and satisfied the need for caution? After all, I'd run this rapid three times before, without incident. Further checking would surely be a waste of time.

Or would it? In a far corner of my mind, I heard the muffled cry of my river angel. Should I heed the call and take time to scout? Longingly, I stared at the blind spot that marked what had always been a clear channel. Then, suddenly, I understood. Time be damned! I would not run this rapid until I checked the chute from the far shore.

Dutifully, I ferried across the prancing rapid and tied up to the gnarled bole of a wind-beaten spruce. Expecting the obvious, I numbly boulder-hopped to the final drop, confident I was in for no surprise. Then I saw it—a two-inch trickle of water marked the vee of the "always canoeable" chute. Horrified at what might have been, I played out the scenario in my mind. Coming out of the fast-forward ferry, we'd spin downstream into nothingness, and capsize in the heavy water that pounded the boulder line below. There simply was not enough water for a clean run!

Silently, I thanked my river angel for her warning, then lined the rapid.

In my travels on the wild rivers of the far north, my river angel has always warned me of the dangers that could lie ahead. If I heed the cry, I come through safely. If not, I often pay a heavy price. Sometimes, my angel tests me with options. Should I attempt the difficult sneak on the right, ride the chest-high rollers at center, or take the chicken route and line or portage? She tests to see if I'm considering all variables, including the skill level of the weakest member of my crew.

I've found my river angel speaks loudest on rivers I haven't done before. On these, I listen best, and so always choose the safest route. Repeat runs, however, require more discipline because her message is muted by past experience and the often-mistaken belief that nothing has changed since I was last there.

My river angel is constant, but fragile; her message can be so easily drowned out by previous success and the shrill of arrogance.

High Water in the Ontario Bush

A T NORMAL WATER LEVELS, the Grand Rapids on the Mattagami River in Ontario are a mile-long stretch of prized whitewater that challenges the skills of intermediate-level canoeists. At least, this is what we were told by a man from Chapleau, Ontario, who had run the river years before.

"Stay near shore," he warned. "Big drops all the way down! The rapid is a mile long and one fourth as wide—you'll be walking home if you capsize in the middle."

Three weeks of steady rain had pushed area rivers over their banks. Ordinarily docile streams were in flood stage and choked with silt. Portages were underwater or otherwise impossible to travel. When we checked in with the Royal Canadian Mounted Police and told them we planned to canoe the Groundhog River to the Mattagami, then continue to James Bay, they put up quite a fuss. "At least wait a few weeks till the water goes down," advised a constable. To emphasize the point, he pulled out a small map of our route and repeatedly tapped his finger on the place where a man had drowned two weeks earlier when his canoe went over a falls. "Had to use grappling hooks to find the body," he said soberly.

Knowing that those who don't canoe don't understand the capabilities of those who do, I remained calm and suggested that the unfortunate victim probably didn't know what he was doing. Then, I tactfully posed the proverbial question, "So you think this high water will make the rapids worse or simply wash 'em out?"

"Probably drown you for sure," the officer said convincingly.

"Don't bet on it!" I muttered under my breath.

My journal from the trip, dated June 11, 1974, reads:

"I'm standing on a small outcrop above Grand Rapids. There's heavy Class II (intermediate level) whitewater far as I can see, and

the mucky banks don't encourage proper scouting. God, will it ever stop raining? I've searched the river with binoculars and can't find a clean route near shore, but the middle looks passable. Left of center looks like the best run, and that's where I want to be. I think."

Avid canoeists may best relate to the uncertainty of the "I think," because in the early seventies, everyone paddled aluminum canoes with big, rock-grabbing t-keels. Mine was an eighteen-foot lightweight Grumman that looked like it had been the focus of a high school ball-peen hammer project. A few good whaps could easily have loosened the age-worn rivets.

I continued to scan the river until I was reasonably certain the run was safe. "C'mon on, Cliff, let's go," prodded the crew impatiently. I exchanged brief glances with my partner, flashed a reluctant smile with a convincing "Okay," then paddled out into the maelstrom. Pity, I was the leader and had to go first.

I remember the run as long and exhilarating, though not particularly difficult. When danger loomed ahead, we simply angled the canoe to the current and paddled backwards. The backferry slowed the craft and moved it across the river with no downstream drift. I don't know what we would have done without this maneuver.

Two-thirds of the way down the rapid, we came upon the torn remains of an American-made Alumacraft canoe that was wrapped securely around a mid-stream boulder. All the gear had been salvaged or had floated free. We wondered about the fate of the paddlers and hoped that, like us, they were a crew of six and could continue on in the remaining two canoes. It was about ninety miles to the town of Moosonee on James Bay—a tough stint for six men in two overloaded canoes. The circumstances suggested that this was a fresh wrap. If the unfortunate paddlers were still on the river, we would probably overtake them.

As we rounded a bend into quiet water, we were surprised to discover a cotton T-shirt tied to a long pole on the river bank. I surmised it marked the location of a cabin and suggested we climb the hill and check it out.

We pulled our canoes well up the mucky bank, tied them to some alders, and sloshed our way through wet vegetation to the top of the embankment where, to our surprise, we discovered a nylon pack that was partially filled with clothing and gear. On top of the pack was a waterproof bottle, inside of which was a note that read:

"June 9: Totalled out in the Grand Rapids on June 2. Canoe lost but salvaged three of four packs. Almost out of food, so hiking east to railroad. Should be there tonight. Please advise authorities of our plight. Please take our pack if you have room."

The names and telephone numbers of two men were printed clearly at the bottom.

I removed the note from the poly bottle and stashed it with my journal, then shouldered the pack and walked back to the canoe. The crew gathered around as we studied the map. It was about eight miles to the rail line—a half-day's hike given normal topography. But this was not "normal" topography. The blue markings on the map indicated the terrain to the east was swamp. There would be no fresh water and no place to camp. It would be difficult or impossible to make a fire. To compound matters, the men would have to cross at least five streams which, given the high water level, would be thundering torrents. I peered through the dark mesh of my head net and listened to the tap tap of hundreds of black flies. The bugs would be even more fierce inland than here!

Why hadn't the pair just built a smoky fire and stayed put? I wondered. We stared again at the map, aware that the men would be lucky to make the tracks at all, let alone in a day.

The following morning, the sky cleared, revealing a brilliant sun. A strong tailwind blew away the bugs and pushed us effortlessly toward the arctic tidewater of Moosonee. We fashioned simple sails, lazed back in the bright warmth, and for the rest of the trip simply steered. We had been on the river fourteen days and it had rained twelve of them. Glory be, sun at last! Anxious for a hot shower, "real" food, and some great Canadian beer, we enthusiastically completed the run to Moosonee in just three days.

Moosonee, Ontario—end of the line for the Ontario Northland railroad. There's a hotel, grocery and liquor store, and a couple of passable eating establishments. A gravel road connects the town with an air force base, train station and city park. A mile across the Moose River is the native community of Moose Factory, where there's a school, clinic and general store, and an interesting tourist museum. Moose Factory is built on permafrost, so water pipes and electrical conduit cannot be buried. A network of huge insulated pipes hover cartoon-like over the town, while downspouts snake into each dwelling.

It was a sweltering 98° (a record!) when we arrived at Moosonee. The train station was less than a mile across town—an easy portage. But we were hot and tired, so we inquired about taxi service. Almost immediately a burly red-haired man drove up in an ancient one-ton truck. "Taxi?" he asked. "You bet," I replied, and in a flash we were loaded and rolling down dusty gravel toward the well-kept station, which marked the end of the line for Ontario Northland's famed "Polar Bear Express." A polished diesel engine with a white polar bear emblazoned boldly on its sides waited in the glaring sun with a team of twenty cars in tow.

There was an Ontario provincial police officer at the station, so I told him about the wrapped canoe and note. He nodded knowingly and told me that two awful looking men had arrived by train two days ago. "They were so bitten up by black flies they had to be hospitalized," said the constable.

We thanked the officer, loaded our gear into the baggage car and retired to the passenger compartment, which was a sweltering 110 degrees! A sweaty, round faced conductor took our tickets and suggested we cool off in the lounge, which was air-conditioned. At that we bolted, knowing the car would be full in a matter of minutes.

Miraculously, there were six unoccupied seats and we took them all. Relieved at last from the heat, bugs and rain, we settled in for the night and round after round of good Canadian beer.

A bond formed immediately when we learned that the two weather-beaten young men who shared our table had also canoed to James Bay. I asked if they'd come by way of the Kapuskasing, Groundhog, or Mattagami River. "Mattagami," came the hesitant reply. At that, I asked them if they'd seen the wrapped canoe and note in the bottle.

"We're the ones who totaled out," said one man meekly. "I don't suppose you guys picked up our pack—we left the car keys in it."

"It's in the baggage car," I reassured him, then I pressed for the details of their story.

The men said they were wearing life jackets when the accident happened, and had no trouble getting out of the water after the canoe capsized and wrapped. They were able to recover three of their four packs, which contained everything except the tent, cooking gear and some food.

For a week, they huddled under a tarp and nursed a fire whose smoke could barely be seen in the persistent rain. To make matters worse, the bugs were awful and they had lost a head net in the capsize. They worked out an agreement whereby each man got to wear the net for an hour.

After a week of sitting around in the bugs and rain, the men could stand it no longer. They had barely two days' supply of food

and were about to lose their sanity, so they decided to hike the eight miles to the railroad. They left the morning of June 9, figuring the walk would take a day.

"It was awful," recalled one of the men. "We were wet to the waist as soon as we started. The swamp just went on and on and on. And every stream was a river that had to be forded."

At night, they huddled under the tarp and prayed the rain would stop. It never did. Each morning they struggled forth again, hopeful they wouldn't have to spend another awful night in the swamp.

By mid-afternoon on the third day, they had reached the tracks, and within the hour the northbound train to Moosonee picked them up. One man was so swollen from bug bites that he required medical help in Moosonee. The men credited their wool garments and rain gear for saving their lives.

After the man was treated at the clinic in Moosonee, the pair took a hotel room, gorged themselves with food, and slept a full twenty hours. Fancy that we should cross paths on the same southbound train. Happily, they both had their health—and their car keys. In return for anonymity, they agreed to pay for all the beer we drank that night—the bill for which, if I recall, came to more than one-hundred Canadian dollars!

A Chippewan Thank-You

SATURDAY IS "TURNAROUND DAY" at many fishing lodges in northern Canada. To take advantage of the morning calm, float planes begin to shuttle fishermen and groceries to and from lodges with the rising sun. By nightfall, the airways are quiet again and everyone is tucked into a spacious cabin and psyched for a week of great fishing and story-telling. After the customary breakfast of Red River cereal and Canadian bacon, clients meet their native guides, who motor them out to hopeful spots where trophy fish lurk. A week later, they fly home, keyed high with tales about the great shore lunches and the lunkers who got away. Of course, these good times would be impossible without the services of the gentle native guides who bait the hooks, clean the fish and service the outboard motors.

Cree Lake Lodge is 180 air miles from LaRonge, Saskatchewan and one-fourth that distance from the nearest Indian settlement. For this reason, many native fishing guides choose to stay with their families in a tent or cabin near the lodge during the tourist season. Once beyond the trailhead, they are completely dependent upon radio telephones and chartered float planes to provide for all their needs. This is the story of a young girl and an aging Chippewan guide whose unique thank-you touched our hearts.

Our intent was to canoe the Cree River from its source at Cree Lake to Stony Rapids on Lake Athabasca. We agreed to supply logistical information about canoeing the Cree, if lodge owner Clarence Biller would provide a night of lodging and pay our air fare from Seeger Lake to his resort. Biller could then share this information with clients who planned to canoe the river.

It was cold and gray and nearly dark when our ancient radial-engined Beaver taxied to the Cree Lake dock. Minutes after the floats touched water, the clouds socked in solid.

Biller greeted us warmly, then asked if there was a doctor aboard. "Yeah," smiled my friend Tom Schwinghamer. "What's up?"

"A little girl—granddaughter of one of my Indian guides—got a splinter in her eye," said Biller. "Too foggy to fly her out and the radio predicts more of the same tomorrow."

"I'll get my kit," said Doc. "You guys better not drink up all the scotch while I'm gone!"

With that, Tom grabbed the medical pack and followed Clarence to a tiny cabin tucked deep in the woods.

As they approached, an expressionless Chippewan man of about seventy swung aside the screen door and motioned them in. The girl, who appeared to be about eight, moaned softly on her cot as Tom approached. Fortunately, the wood shard had missed the eye, but it was dangerously close. Tom smiled and talked quietly to the girl as he pulled a needle from his kit and injected a local anesthetic. Though it must have been terribly painful, the youngster did not fidget or scream. Seconds later, the splinter was out and the eye was patched. Tom handed a small bottle of pills to the girl's mother, along with some instructions for the child's care. Then, he patted the little girl's hand and told her she'd be okay. As he rose to leave, the elderly grandfather—who had said nothing during the operation—nodded an unemotional thank-you.

The next morning, when we were getting ready to leave, I saw the grandfather again. He walked quietly to the dock and for a while just watched while I carried packs through the cabin door and stacked them by a tree. Then, without a word, he grabbed a pack and carried it to the dock. He continued helping us until all twelve of our packs were neatly stacked on the wharf. Then he helped us carry our canoes to the water. Never once did he say anything.

When the canoes were finally loaded, he smiled broadly and held up his hand in a fond good-bye. Then he turned quietly and shuffled back to the cabin and his still-sleeping granddaughter. Though nothing was said, the experience touched me deeply. Every one of us could feel the old man's deep, heartfelt thanks for the kindness Tom had shown his granddaughter.

I set my compass for a bearing through the fog, then paddled alongside Tom's red Old Town Tripper canoe. "Great day to start a canoe trip," he called. I looked into the gentle moistness of his eyes, and replied, "You bet!"

John and Martha

QUICK! NAME THE ONE THING that an adult most fears about camping in the backcountry with an ordinary group of fifteen-year-old boys and girls? If you said bears or bad weather, you're dead wrong. A broken leg, death by fiery lightning, getting lost in the boonies . . . those aren't highest on the list either.

What's most feared is love—google-eyed, heart-throbbing, hormone-pumping, toe-tripping puppy love. If you want a supreme challenge, pair up two enamored teenagers on your next wilderness outing. Then, see if you can solve all the problems they'll create.

Fortunately, you can avoid the scenario by administering a simple test to identify potential troubles. Here's how it works: Say you've agreed to lead a church-sponsored canoe trip down a local river. Sixteen kids—eight boys, eight girls—have signed up and are chomping at the bit. Logistics (and your own sanity) demand that you split the group into two smaller crews of nine. You'll chaperone one group, another adult will guide the other. Be aware that teenagers are social animals that travel in close-knit packs. Separate buddies and many of the kids will drop out. The idea is to pair good friends, but not lovers. To discern the difference, have the youngsters write down the names of their close friends and arch enemies. Use the data to make up your groups, taking care to split friends of the opposite sex. What could be simpler? I thought I'd done a good job of separating potential troublemakers when I placed John and Martha—who apparently were not interested in one another—in the same group.

Unfortunately, I learned too late that the kids knew how my "sociogram" worked. They outfoxed the system by pretending they were casual peers.

Problems surfaced the first night out. As soon as we pitched camp, John asked Martha to join him on a distant rock where he would show her the mechanics of spin-casting. On the third try, her reel (which was evidently not locked down properly) went flying out into the lake. The line snapped and the unit plunged into the deep. When the embarrassment subsided, Martha apologized to John, whereupon John borrowed another reel from a friend, who made him promise that if he lost it, he'd buy it. John wanted to prove to his friend that the reel wouldn't let go, so he cast the lure with all his might. At this, the rod tip pulled loose, snapped the line, and flew into the lake. The fishing scene ended abruptly with a compassionate, "Awww . . . John."

Oblivious to the comedy they had created, the pair nonchalantly strolled back to camp, where John presented me with a novel idea. "There's gobs of crawdads down by the shore. Whatcha say we cook some up for supper?"

"Ever cook a mess of crawdads?" I asked.

"Yeah, sure, do it all the time!"

"Okay," I said. "Go for it!"

John made a crude net out of his T-shirt and trapped about three dozen of the little buggers. He boiled them up in salted water and served them, taking care to remove the tiny "mud" vein. The crayfish were surprisingly good and the episode put John back into Martha's good graces.

Early the next day, it began to rain. The kids knew they were supposed to pack their foul weather gear under a pack flap so they could reach it easily. But Martha had forgotten the rules; her parka was at the bottom of her pack. I was about to reprimand her for the oversight when John handed his rain suit to her, saying in a hushed tone, "Here, Martha, you can wear mine."

"So what are you gonna wear?" I queried. "My wool lumberjack coat," came the reply. It was a warm rain and there was no danger of hypothermia, so I reluctantly nodded okay. Maybe the episode would teach them both a lesson.

The rain quit a few hours later, and bright sunlight flooded the day. Hungry and eager to dry out, we put ashore on an airy point and broke out lunch. John wrung out his checkered wool jacket and draped it over a sun warmed boulder, then he and Martha sat down together on a damp cedar log. Almost immediately, Martha stood up and cried, "Aw, John, my butt's all wet!"

"Here, sit on my life jacket," said John, apologetically. Martha smiled coyly and beamed. " Thanks, Johnny," she cooed.

I thought no more about the incident until we were back in the canoes and paddling down a placid beaver stream. It was a sweltering 94°, so I succumbed to pressure and agreed to let the kids take off their life jackets. Three portages later, we emerged on a large lake and I told the kids to put the vests back on. Everyone but John complied.

"Buckle up, John," I scolded.

"I can't. Uh, I think I lost it," he gloomily replied. Then he told me he'd left it on the log at our lunch spot four lakes back. I told John he was fortunate he was on the swim team, and could probably live without it. But, "You *will* pay for it!" I chided.

The next morning was chilly, so everyone broke out warm clothes. Everyone, that is, except John. Generally, I don't like to pester kids about their personal attire, but it was obvious that John was cold, so I asked him why he didn't put on his red lumberjack shirt.

"I think I lost it," he muttered dolefully. "Hung it on a rock after the rain and, uh, I guess I forgot it."

"Well, you've got your rain gear; why don't you put that on?" I suggested.

"Uh . . . " At this, Martha chimed in, "I lost his jacket, Mr. J. Got the pants though!" Then she told me she had left the parka on the damp cedar log they had shared the day before.

By now, John and Martha had become a major source of entertainment for everyone, and the crew needled the pair constantly. It was the fifth day of our canoe trip and John had already lost a fishing rod tip, reel, wool jacket, rain parka and life vest. Before the day was out, he would also lose his flashlight.

Shortly after sundown, Martha discovered that the switch on her flashlight had somehow been turned on while the unit was in her pack. The batteries were stone dead. So she strolled over to John's tent, batted her eyes, and asked if she could borrow his flashlight to go to the bathroom.

"Sure, sure, Martha, you keep it," he said tenderly. She did, and promptly misplaced it! John became despondent as he realized he would have to explain the losses to his mom and dad. So, at the campfire that night, everyone got into the act by suggesting ways that he could save face when he told his parents. Martha felt particularly sorry for John, so she tried to cheer him up by showing off her new dance routine on the bole of a huge downed tree. It worked, and John burst into laughter, but then Martha fell off the log and sprained her ankle. Now, she could could not carry anything over the portages—poor John would have to haul it all! To make matters worse, we were in a very remote area, where portages were just minutes apart.

John did everything for Martha. The instant the canoe touched shore, he was out, knee-deep in water. Martha would put her arms around his neck and he would carry her ashore, where she would hobble over the portage trail with the aid of her makeshift crutch. Then, John would single-handedly unload the canoe and portage the gear across. Of course, the other kids offered to help, but John politely refused. He was a big strapping boy and wanted to show off his muscles to Martha.

Six hours and eight portages later, the tremendous physical labor began to take its toll. John was tired. Very tired. The final straw fell at a mucky portage on the edge of a foul-smelling swamp. It was about 100° in the glaring sun and the mosquitoes were God-awful. Sweat rolled off John's body in waves as he struggled with the heavy packs. Everyone was dying of thirst and anxious for a swim, but the dank swamp water was unfit for both. Thick "lob-lolly" mud began at the shoreline and stretched tirelessly down the portage trail. The kids groaned under the wilting weight of the packs and canoes, and wished they were somewhere else.

Finally, the packs were across and John returned for his canoe. He edged out to the boat to a rotten log, flipped the canoe onto his shoulders and wheeled to face the portage trail. But the canoe caught firmly in the branches of a large black spruce, and refused to budge. Sweating and straining, John bit his lip so he wouldn't swear, while in the background, Martha leaned on her crutch and shouted directions.

"Turn right, no left. Back up a bit. Go forward. More. More!" Then, without warning, John slid off the log into the murky water. Still holding the canoe overhead, he sank deeper and deeper into the oozing muck. Soon, he was waist-deep and solidly stuck. Unable to move, he suppressed what I interpreted as an intent to swear, and with brute force, threw the canoe into the swamp. It landed with a loud splat, and a shower of mud. Then, it drifted just out of reach. Now, the only way to get it back was to swim for it. John glared at Martha, stiffly cooing, "Awww gee, Martha." Then he slipped into the foul water and dog-paddled toward the canoe.

Seconds later, he emerged from the swamp like a sluggish dinosaur, and in a barely controlled voice said, "Awww . . . Martha." As he turned to face her, she burst out laughing, at which he turned beet-red, clenched his fists and at the top of his lungs bellowed, "Dammit, Martha, I hate you!" This was their first and last domestic squabble. In a flash the romance was over—John and Martha had become "just friends."

For some unaccountable reason, I refused to admonish John for his ill-mannered outburst. Justice was on the wind at last, and I felt it was best to leave it at that.

Don't Worry Doc! We'll Make It.

by Erik Watt

Erik Watt is a politically incorrect misfit who fled North after thirty years as a fourth-generation newsman. He's been in Canada's Northwest Territories since he was a teenaged Mackenzie River deck hand in 1943. He was a southern-based reporter on the North from 1956 to 1962. He arrived in Yellowknife in 1976, and put in seven years as director of public affairs for Indian and Northern Affairs in Canada's Northwest Territories Region. He's been a writer and media consultant since1985.

Erik is the author of Yellowknife: How A City Grew *(Outcrop Ltd., 1990), and* McDougall's Bash, *a collection of Northern Poetry (Outcrop Ltd., 1993). His article,* Don't Worry Doc! We'll Make It, *first appeared in the October/November, 1992 issue of* Up Here: Life In Canada's North *magazine. It is the heart-warming story of Jim McAvoy—a daredevil Canadian bush pilot who carved history with his wings. I love the story and know you will too.—C.J.*

IN FORTY-THREE YEARS of flying in the North, Jim McAvoy has become a figure of legend. And in Jim's case, that legend is based solidly on fact.

There's an aviation maxim that says there are lots of old pilots and lots of bold pilots, but not many old, bold pilots. Jim is one of that rare breed, still flying a Single Otter out of Yellowknife Bay, still turning his intimate knowledge of lakes, bush and barrens into smooth landings in places nobody else would attempt.

He's a pilot of many reputations, not the least of which has been his uncanny ability to find and rescue people in distress. He's also known as a superb flyer with a devilish sense of humour, a fierce battler of red tape, and—in his early years at least—a good-natured hell-raiser of heroic proportions.

These days, Jim resists the temptation to buzz anything he sees moving below. But if he has a friend aboard, he's not above enlivening a dull flight by waiting until the engine of his Single Otter starves to a stop before switching to his reserve fuel tank.

"He gets me every time," growls Bill Tait, a Yellowknife tourist operator. "We'll be chugging along, and all of a sudden there's this awful quiet and we're going down.

"You can switch from the main tank to the reserve tank on an Otter, but you can't switch back. Usually, Jim makes the switch while he still has fuel in the main tank, but not when he has me as a passenger! I guess he likes to see the look on my face when the engine quits!"

McAvoy has perhaps forty-thousand flying hours under his belt, but nowadays, Ministry of Transport regulations are severely cutting into his flying time. The rules keep airline pilots from flying more than about 80 hours a month.

"I can remember one summer putting in 642 hours in 15 weeks," McAvoy says. "That's more than a lot of pilots do in six months nowadays."

No wonder rules irritate Jim; he's used to operating on his own excellent instincts. Yellowknifers used to know winter was over for sure the day Jim McAvoy ambled out on the ice of Back Bay to his deHavilland Beaver, and flew the six miles to Long Lake, where he'd switch his ski-wheels for floats. His was always the last plane off the ice.

Today, we know summer has arrived when Jim and his co-pilot Salty—a five-year-old toy poodle—drive into town in the RV that's their summer home. They head for CF-CZP, a venerable Single Otter parked at Air Tindi's Old Town float base. Jim McAvoy—and no one else—will fly CZP until the season's finished.

McAvoy sold Latham Island Island Airways, his Yellowknife-based float and ski charter company, in 1978, allegedly to retire to an acreage he and his wife, Betty, bought near Edmonton. He was back in Yellowknife and flying again by the following spring, and he's been doing it ever since.

Jim and Salty haul tourists, trappers, fishermen, geologists, prospectors and their supplies all over the western Northwest Territories until freeze-up, in September or October. Salty hates flying, but he hates being left behind even more. "If it gets a little rough he'll dash back and hide in the tail compartment," says Jim.

Jim McAvoy first arrived in Yellowknife in the spring of 1944, when it was a ten-year-old mining town with a population of less than four-thousand. Fort Smith, not Yellowknife, was the unofficial territorial capital in those days, and our town was barely hanging in, its gold mines shut down by the wartime labor shortage. But mining exploration never stops, and many a husky teenager was filling the boots of the men off to war.

Jim, a 14-year-old farm boy, had come North to join his father, Jim McAvoy Sr., a well-known territorial prospector and mining developer, in the bush. His first work was as a helper to shaft miners and diamond drillers at a small mine his father developed northeast of Yellowknife.

"I was nearly always out in the bush after that," Jim recalls. "I worked as a staker and prospector, and I did a lot of drilling and trenching (sampling surface showings) all over the place."

He insists he got into flying "because I hated walking," and, quite literally, by accident.

"By 1948, Dad had fourteen or fifteen camps spread all over the western Northwest Territory, and he had real problems keeping them supplied. Aircraft were hard to charter in the summer—you sometimes had to book two weeks ahead because they were so busy. So Dad decided he had to get a plane of his own."

Jim Sr. had a close pal with deHavilland Aircraft in Toronto. He persuaded deHaviland to resume production of its biplane Fox Moth, a prewar bush plane that had done well in the North. He took delivery of three Fox Moths, and one after the other, they were written off in crashes. In desperation, the father sent young Jim south to Edmonton to learn to fly.

Jim got his commercial license in March, 1949, and flew planes for McAvoy Diamond Drilling, West Bay Mining, and his father's other companies until Jim Sr.'s death in 1953.

After that, McAvoy flew for outfits like Gateway Aviation, Carter Aviation in Hay River, Koenen Air Service, or anyone else who needed a pilot with his own plane. He had no trouble finding work; he'd built himself a solid reputation as a pilot by then. And there was always prospecting to fall back on.

Whenever things were quiet he'd be off to check out prospects he'd noted from the air. (He and prospector-pilot Joe Herriman discovered gold in the Indian Lake area, site of the now-suspended Colomac Mine.)

Jim's younger brother, Chuck, had also become a pilot, and in 1960 Jim and Chuck teamed up to form McAvoy Air Services, based in Yellowknife. They had four single-engined aircraft—an ancient Fairchild 82, survivor of the pioneer years of bush flying; two STOL (short takeoff and landing) Helio couriers; and a Cessna 180, all on floats or skis.

That enterprise lasted just a year; the brothers McAvoy had their differences. Chuck kept the company, and Jim struck out on his own.

On June 9, 1964, Chuck, the old Fairchild and two prospectors vanished without a trace on a flight to Izok Lake, east of Great Bear.

"Jim flew more hours on that search than anyone else," says Glenn Warner of Yellowknife, an ex-Mountie and friend of both brothers. "Every inch of that area was checked out. We never found anything. The weather was poor, and the best guess is that the Fairchild iced up and went straight to the bottom of a lake."

It wasn't just in the air that Jim McAvoy made his name in that era. Yellowknife was a hard-drinking town, and no one loved a good party—or a good fight—better than the soft-spoken, good-natured and burly Jim McAvoy.

Oldtimers still recall with awe the nights when young Jim McAvoy decided to flex his muscles. The Gold Range Cafe, next door to the rip-roaring Gold Range bar, was his favorite spot. Almost invariably, someone would wind up flying through the cafe's big plate-glass window, and the whole Royal Canadian Mounted Police detachment would be called out to restore order.

Next morning, Jim would apologize to everyone, commiserate with the casualties, pay his fine and settle the cafe's damage bill. And Yellowknife would heave a sigh of relief, until next time.

"Jim was never a mean drunk," says long-time Yellowknifer Smokey Heal, an old crony. "But he sure did love to fight!"

McAvoy's marriage to Betty McChesney, who'd come North in 1946 when her father went to work at the Beaulieu Mine east of Yellownife, probably pleased no one more than the Gold Range's proprietors. And Betty, who often flew with him, quickly proved her mettle.

She was with Jim that day in 1958, when he decided to fly under the Yellowknife Highway bridge at Frank's Channel, one-hundred kilometers east of Yellowknife. Great Slave Lake's well-treed North Arm is pretty narrow at that point, and the bridge's high end is just 12 meters off the water. Jim is pretty indignant about the persistent story that he looped the bridge. "I only flew under it," he protests. "Both ways."

There is no shortage of eyewitness accounts of his favorite sport of that era: swooping down silently, prop idling, on unsuspecting Cat operators, prospectors or road-builders out in the middle of nowhere. He would then open the throttle wide and thunder past, over their heads.

"I remember once catching four guys working with pluggers (gas-operated rock drills) on a piece of highway right-of-way," McAvoy grins. "When I looked back, all I could see was the four pluggers, still banging away by themselves. The crew was flat on their bellies in the bush!"

Not surprisingly, McAvoy proved to be a constant burr under the Department of Transportation's saddle.

He knew exactly the payload any aircraft he flew could get off the ground, and that was often well above the Department of Transport's load limits. He knew how long it would take to get from A to B, and how to get into C with fog hanging in the trees, and to heck with Department of Transport minimums. He knew the capabilities of the aircraft he flew better than the people who'd designed them. In an emergency, with every other aircraft grounded by weather, people knew Jim McAvoy would somehow get through.

Jim McAvoy has always liked to fly low, watching the terrain below him with a prospector's keen eye, slipping down for a closer look if a rock formation attracted his interest, often landing to check it out. In the process, he's learned how to get in and out of impossibly small or shallow lakes and sloughs.

In 1958, I flew with Jim in his fully loaded Cessna 180 to a highway construction camp on a drought-shrunken pothole lake southwest of Fort Rae. I held my breath as he literally flew the plane to the shore, his floats barely skimming the surface once we touched down. Just when it appeared we were going to wind up in the camp cookhouse, Jim chopped the throttle.

We came to a swift stop three meters from the dock, floats high and dry. When we got set to leave, the camp crew had to haul us out to the middle of the lake with a tracked Nodwell vehicle so we'd be in enough water to float us for takeoff.

Two weeks later, he flew J.E. "Doc" Savage, then the Northwest Territories' supervising highways engineer for the Department of Public Works, in and out of the same lake. The weather had stayed hot and dry and the lake, by then, was even smaller.

They skimmed into shore, but McAvoy ran right out of lake on return takeoff. In the instant before the floats charged up onto the muskeg, McAvoy turned to Doc Savage and grinned.

"Don't worry, Doc!" he said. "We'll make it!"

And they did, though they skipped over the muskeg for a hundred meters or so before Jim got enough speed up to yank the Cessna into the air and clear the trees.

McAvoy earned his reputation as a spotter of people in trouble below because he's constantly scrutinizing the ground as he flies. He doesn't miss much, and on several occasions he's found people before anyone knew they were missing.

One of McAvoy's best-known exploits was his 1958 rescue of three people forced down north of Fort Rae when their two aircrafts became lost and they ran out of fuel. One pilot managed to walk out for help, but by the time a search plane had located the downed planes, the lake on which they'd landed had frozen over.

The ice was too thin to support a plane, and too thick for floats. The situation was dire, since one of the stranded people, wildlife biologist George Hunter, had developed a critical infection. His wife was preparing to amputate his hand in a desperate effort to save his life.

The search plane flew back to Yellowknife, where the Royal Canadian Air Force search-master called a hasty meeting to discuss the crisis. There were no helicopters closer than Ontario, and by the time one could be flown up, or a ground party could get to George Hunter, it would be too late.

No one invited Jim McAvoy to that meeting; he was grounded after one of his many run-ins with the Department of Transport. But he had heard about Hunter's grim plight quickly enough. And while the emergency meeting was being assembled, Jim quietly took off from ice-free Yellowknife Bay in his Cessna, and headed north.

An hour later, he was examining the lake on which the party was stranded. By then, darkness wasn't far off.

McAvoy made his decision quickly. He made one low pass across the lake, bouncing his floats on the ice to smash it. Then he swung around, landed in the ice-choked, perilously narrow channel he'd created, picked up the stranded trio and took off again—miraculously without piercing his floats.

Hunter was admitted to the hospital in Yellowknife before the emergency meeting ended, and he was out of danger a week later. DOT didn't press any more charges against McAvoy. Not just then, at any rate.

McAvoy was famous, too, for the mountain searches in which he participated. More than one observer who flew with him recalls with terror that Jim was the only pilot who'd search blind canyons too narrow to turn around in and too deep to climb out of.

As the granite walls of a canyon converged, McAvoy would haul back on the wheel and pull his aircraft up into a loop, rolling off the loop at the top. Then he'd fly serenely back the way he'd come.

Looping in float planes is not exactly recommended, but Jim McAvoy always knew what his plane could do, and he always survived. His keen eyesight proved to be no blessing a few years ago, though.

McAvoy was flying a single-engined Maule equipped with skis, heading for Fort Simpson after a trip into the Nahanni, when he saw a man waving frantically on the breaking ice of Little Doctor Lake. There was a lot of open water along the shore and the remaining ice looked shaky. But McAvoy wasn't going to leave someone in serious danger, if he could help it.

One section of the ice, near the man, appeared fairly good. McAvoy set the Maule down and slid about sixty meters before the ice collapsed. His plane hung up by its wings long enough for him to scramble out.

The man came running, vastly relieved to find McAvoy soaked, but alive. "Thought you were going to try to land," he gasped, "and I was trying to wave you off. This ice is in terrible shape!" So was the Maule, resting on the lake bottom. Jim had loved that little plane, but he settled for the insurance.

McAvoy had his share of closer calls.

In 1967, he and Betty flew to the Cadillac silver mine's landing strip, near Nahanni National Park. He landed on wheels on a sandbar at the bottom of deep Prairie Creek Canyon, where turbulence is often fierce. Just before touchdown, the throttle cable of the Helio Courier broke, leaving Jim without power.

The radio operator at the strip, unable to see around a bend that masked approaching aircraft until the last seconds, was just about to panic when Jim's voice came over the radio.

"You'd better come and get me," Jim said. "I'm about 350 feet short of the runway."

He'd come down on the boulder-strewn bank of the creek, but neither he, Betty nor the Helio Courier had sustained serious damage.

Jim McAvoy's closest call came a year later, when he landed near the east end of Great Slave Lake to pick up prospector Gus Weyrowitz. They'd just lifted off the water when McAvoy's controls froze. The Helio Courier stood on its tail and climbed four-hundred feet before stalling. Then it fell back into the frigid lake.

"It didn't seem that hard on impact," he remembers today. "We landed right-side-up. But the impact wrecked the undercarriage, and smashed one float."

The aircraft remained afloat long enough for McAvoy to get off a Mayday call, which no one heard. Then, as the Helio Courier slowly rolled over and began to sink, McAvoy and Weyrowitz jumped clear and dragged themselves up on the one intact float, still attached to the now-sunken fuselage.

The date was June 9, 1968—four years to the day after Chuck McAvoy's disappearance.

Much of Great Slave was still ice-choked, and the water was only a degree or two above freezing. McAvoy and Weyrowitz had been able to grab life jackets and a sleeping bag before the fuselage went under, but small, ice-cold waves kept splashing over the float to which they clung.

They'd crashed just before 1 P.M. By late afternoon, when McAvoy should have been back in Yellowknife, a search was being organized. One of the search planes flew right over them around 9 P.M. but didn't see them, and another came fairly close around midnight. By then, the wind was picking up and currents were carrying the submerged aircraft father away from shore.

"That was a miserable night," McAvoy recalls. "It got cold when the sun went down (around midnight) and the waves started breaking over us. There were three-foot swells."

They'd had nothing to eat, and sleep was impossible; they had to stay awake to avoid being swept off the float. "All we could do was sit there and hang on."

Two more aircraft flew over them as daylight returned, says Jim. "But it's hard to spot something as small as we were. After that, I guess Gus just gave up hope. He started slipping off the float. The first couple of times I helped him get back on, but the third time he didn't even try. I managed to pull him up, but he died half an hour later."

It was 3 P.M. on Monday when pilot Brock "Rocky" Parsons of Northwest Territorial Airways spotted the wreckage, landed and plucked shivering Jim McAvoy and his dead passenger's body from the float.

Three hours later, a Department of Transport investigative team flew down the East Arm to examine the wrecked aircraft. It had completely disappeared.

The water tower that once stood on the rocky hilltop in Old Town, where Yellowknife's Bush Pilots' Monument now points skyward, is long gone now. Nor is it likely that Jim McAvoy, today, would still use it to check his vision and reflexes, as he did in the early years.

Back then, Jim would see how close to the tank he could come with his wing tip every time he took off. He'd be in a bad mood all day if he missed it by more than a foot.

Jim McAvoy doesn't need to prove himself to himself any more, nor to anyone else. And Salty doesn't care. All he wants to do is get one more flight behind him, as the Otter's floats slice through the sparkling water of Yellowknife Bay and then lift into the Northern sky Jim McAvoy knows and loves so well.

Glossary of Terms

Canoeing Terms:

Backferry: Canoeists use this procedure to cross strong currents without slipping downstream. Essentially, the canoe is turned about 30 degrees to the current and paddled backward.

Crossdraw: A crossover stroke used by the bow paddler of a canoe to turn the boat quickly away from his or her normal paddling side.

Cutwater: The place on the curve of the bow and stern of the canoe that is just out of the water.

Freeboard: The distance from the water line to the top of the lowest point of the gunnels of the canoe. Usually, the greater the freeboard, the greater the ability of the canoe to handle rough water.

Haystacks: Large standing waves in a river, which indicate deep water and "safe" canoeing.

Horsetails: The huge, dancing waves of a rapid.

Kevlar™: A very strong, lightweight honey-gold fabric developed by the DuPont Company; used to build the best canoes, among other things.

Line: Rope used to tie up a canoe, or pull it around obstacles in the water. Also refers to working a canoe downstream around obstacles in the water with the aid of ropes (lines) attached to the bow and stern.

Portage: To carry a canoe and gear overland, either to a distant watershed or to safer water. "Carry" is synonymous with portage.

Rock fans: An accumulation of shallow rocks at the base of a rapid. Rock fans may stretch for hundreds of yards. Often, there is not enough water between the rocks for a canoe to safely pass.

Royalex™: An exceptionally strong thermoplastic laminate developed by the Uniroyal™ Company. The toughest whitewater canoes are constructed of Royalex™.

Souseholes: A large volume of water that flows over a huge rock may create a dangerous sousehole at the base of the rock. Souseholes actually are eddies standing on edge. The whirlpool-like currents that form at the base of a big sousehold can trap and hold a canoe.

Stern pry: A combination rudder and outward pry applied by the stern (back) person in a canoe. A stern pry turns the canoe smartly away from the stern person's paddling side.

Sweeper: A downed tree that partially or completely blocks the river's flow. Sweepers are among the most dangerous obstacles in canoeing.

Thwart: A cross-brace that runs across the canoe.

Tumpline: A strap that is secured just above a person's forehead to help support a pack or canoe. The early Voyageurs carried everything on tumplines.

Wind-bound: When high winds make a lake too rough to canoe, the wise canoeist simply hangs around and waits for better weather.

Yoke: A special cross-brace equipped with shoulder pads that is used to carry a canoe.

Other terms:

Esker: A ridge of gravel or sand likely formed by streams under or in glacial ice.

Inuit: The native (preferred) name for Eskimo.

Muskeg: A Canadian (or North American) bog.

Sic sic: A Canadian ground squirrel.

Tote road: A rough, gravel road used to service logging or mining operations.